"Author and speaker, Kathyrn Ann Murray is affectionatly known as "Kit" to so many. She has a life signature like no other. Out of life's pain, and gained wisdom, she sings a song of JOY and dances in that freedom.

Kit reminds us that God is not only LOVE, He is certainly JOY too!"

Rev. Judy Shaw
Spiritual Leader and Global Speaker
March 2018

The Chaos Eaters

Overcoming Chaos Addiction and achieving an Authentic Self

Kathryn Murray

ISBN: 978-1-945255-97-7

All rights reserved. No part of this book may be reproduced or transmitted in any form or by any means, electronic or mechanical, including photocopying, recording or by any information storage and retrieval system, without permission in writing from the copyright owner. For information on distribution rights, royalties, derivative works, or licensing opportunities on behalf of this content or work, please contact the publisher at the address below.

Printed in the United States of America.

Layout Design and Editor: Shelley Furtado-Linton

Although the author and publisher have made every effort to ensure that the information and advice in this book was correct and accurate at press time, the author and publisher do not assume and hereby disclaim any liability to any party for any loss, damage, or disruption caused from acting upon the information in this book or by errors or omissions, whether such errors or omissions result from negligence, accident, or any other cause.

Chaos Eaters

CONTENTS

	Preface	i
	Preface to CHAOS EATERS	ii
1	What is Chaos?	5
2	Where Does the Appetite for Chaos Come From?	9
3	Personality: Stepping Stone or Stumbling Block?	19
4	Shame: The Petrie Dish of Dysfunction.	43
5	The Intra-Personal Dynamics of Shame	53
6	Shame-Fear-Control	63
7	Offense: The Go to Jail Free Card	69
8	Offense Will Come	83
9	Establishing a Language of Recovery	89
10	My Story: Everyone Has One	99
11	Fatherlessness: Attempting Life Without the Father's Blessing	115
12	What is, IS! What isn't, ISN'T!	131
13	Unknown, Red Light, Green Light, and Flashing Yellow	137
14	Without Revelation We Are Unrestrained	141
15	The Kingdom of God Is Not A Kingdom Of Chaos	155
	Epilogue	161

PREFACE

"This is a small book of mustard seeds, plant them and they will grow into great trees of understanding"
Kathryn Murray

At the outset of my introduction to this book I will reveal that I have been a woman's minister for almost twenty years. Most of the information and topics that will be approached in this material come out of the experiences I have had as a minister. I have spent time ministering, counseling, and trying to understand the complex nature of interpersonal dynamics.

Trying to discover what works and what doesn't work and what seems to be bedrock in human relationships. But more than that, I am a woman and I am by nature a relational creation; the relational nuances of communication and relationship are really a woman's nature. I believe that women, as a sex, are hard wired to be communicators and relational beings. And for this reason alone, women have a natural skill set and desire to see below the surface of things.

Women naturally get the under currents and structural dynamics of communication and understanding (and misunderstanding). Where ever women gather I think you will find a natural lab to study human dynamics. I am also a sister. I was the first of four daughters raised in a primarily matriarchal home environment which gave me invaluable firsthand experience in the female psyche.

I have seen firsthand how important it is for women to get relationships right and how damaging and corrosive wrong relationships are to a woman's soul. And yes, I believe that we all do have a soul; the mind, will and emotional center in each of us where we think, feel, and find our motivations to act. This book will be a distillation of many years of experience; living and being engaged in the very real and difficult enterprise to understand my own relational intentions and those of others.

This will not be a psychological treatise in any way, although there will be psychological constructs introduced. This book will not be a scriptural exegesis although biblical principles will be presented. I am neither a psychologist nor a theologian; I am a woman whose life experience and desire to understand my own motivations and actions has led me to some foundational principals. I have constructed an affirming and positive personal and interpersonal understanding of the nature of communication and importance of relationships not only in my life but in the lives of others.

Put simply, I have found that some things work and some things never will never work in relationships.

I have read a lot of books on the subjects that will be presented here. I have sat under some insightful and profound training on the topics. And although, I have read many great books and sat under some insightful teaching, I have learned the most empowering principals through trial and error, just by living life intentionally and listening to the stories of my fellow travelers along the way.

Chaos Eaters

None of us are immune from the feelings and constructs that come from living a life; good, bad, or indifferent. It is incumbent that each of us find a process to free us from the tyranny of bad education, training and our own personal demons of shame, guilt, rejection, abandonment, and chaos addiction. We need to be equipped for such an undertaking.

We need materials that will support that journey. I am hopeful that this little book will be such a resource. I know I would have been grateful for such a resource as I was finding my own way to these principals.

This book is as much a journal of recovery as it is a manual to introduce some healthful, life and relational principals to help build constructive, graceful, and affirming relationships and communities. It really represents what I know up to this point about these matters. But I find that so many of the topics I will address here still remain undiscovered or underappreciated by so many individuals that I meet in my life; not only in my ministry but in the day to day interactions with so many whose paths I cross.

I guess at a time in my life when leaving a legacy is an important to me; I want to leave this book as a testament to the widest possible audience I can hope to attract.

Please read this book with and open heart, my prayer is that you will find some answers on these pages.

CHAPER ONE: WHAT IS CHAOS?

"There is an obsolete word that describes chaos; it is translated chasm. A chasm is a great, yawning hole in the ground which seemingly has no bottom"
 Kathryn Murray

The definition of chaos would sure make it seem to be something to be avoided. The dictionary defines chaos as a state of utter confusion and disorder; a great state of commotion, disturbance, tumult, agitation, and convulsion and upheaval. It is the state of being in a harassing uproar.

It can also present itself as a violent and noisy disturbance or a turbulent and emotional state of mind. Who in their right mind would entertain such a state of consciousness or allow such a state of affairs to exist in their life? It makes no real sense that people actually entertain such a state of chaos in their lives but they do.

Look into your own life, where have you made place for confusion, upheaval, agitation, and disturbance? We don't examine these raiders into our peace and wellbeing enough.

We often just coexist with them allowing those forces to destroy our own peace of mind, sense of wellbeing and health and our relationships.

There is an obsolete word that describes chaos; it is translated, chasm. A chasm is great, yawning hole in the ground which seemingly has no bottom.

And I confess sometimes I have entertained chaos and felt like I had dropped into that bottomless pit. What despair and hopelessness does such a chasm represent to you? Not anything that we would willingly jump into but we find ourselves gripped sometimes by an attraction to that hole in the ground.

We are drawn to it by the pull of unexamined and powerful forces within our own hearts or relationships that ensnare us into compromising our own best interest and common sense." Why do I do the things I do?" we may ask ourselves without really having any idea on how to answer that question. It seems so ingrained in who we are that the characteristics of chaos may be how we define ourselves; resigned to the status quo of terrible agitation, confusion, disorder, and brokenness.

So, what is there in us that draws us to Chaos? There must be a power in chaos that keeps us coming back for more, even when we know that our best interests are not served by the association.

Part of the attraction of chaos may be that it is a quickener of SENSATION. Think of it this way, if you feel numb inside and empty; chaos infuses you with a rush of feelings and a quickening of your emotions. It can be a rush so to speak and even though it is not good for you it is like a drug which gives you a momentary heightened sense of yourself. It seems better than the alternative which is emptiness and blankness.

It also feeds into the inner expectations that what we think we deserve from life.

If our life experiences have been negative and painful and destructive, we can feel that chaos and its attendant miseries are all we are worthy of and all that we can expect out of life. So strangely by letting chaos run havoc in our lives we are actually reinforcing our core beliefs of what we are worthy of. There is a perverted logic in that and even a distorted sense of satisfaction that what you believe to be true about living actually, from your point of view and ongoing experience, is true.

What is also true about Chaos is that while being a quickener of SENSATION; Chaos is not a servant of SENSE, OR ORDER, OR PEACE, and OR DISCIPLINE OR YOUR BEST INTERESTS. And we all know that deep down inside although we seem powerless to overcome the grip and attraction that Chaos has on our lives, we still hope for a remedy.
We continue to make the same sad choices and fall deeper and deeper into confusion, agitation, and disorder. Why do we allow this? There are many reasons and we are going to explore the cause and effect of Chaos in the next chapters of this book.

QUESTIONS

What despair or hopelessness does the chasm (chaos) in your life represent to you?

What emotions does chaos bring up for you?

What choices have you continued to make that have caused you to remain in chaos?

CHAPTER TWO: WHERE DOES THE APPETITE FOR CHAOS COME FROM?

"Many of us realize that we continue to make decisions that run contrary to our own best interests. And yet we are seemingly powerless to affect long term change despite our best intentions and fervent resolution to be different. Many of us feel a lot like Sisyphus, the Greek character who was condemned by the gods to continually roll a huge stone up a mountain only to have it rollback on us after we had painstakingly pushed it to the top. WE FEEL CONDEMNED TO REPEAT THE SAME AWFUL PATTERNS AND PURPOSELESS ACTIONS WITHOUT ANY HOPE OF CHANGE."
 Kathryn Murray

I believe that each of us needs a peaceful center for our lives in order to live up to our full potential. There are so many studies now about the relationship between dis-ease and stress on the human psychology and physiology. It is no longer a theory that there is a direct correlation between stresses and diseases such a hypertension and cancer and psychological conditions like chronic depression. The body, spirit and soul are designed to flourish in a positive, life-affirming, and peaceful environment.

Negative influences which destroy that desired and proscribed environment work against our health and best interests in short term and long term. If the stress is unique and atypical the affect is not as great as stress which is sustained and habitual.

Long term constant stress will produce long term disastrous results and patterns of behavior which cause us to perpetuate stress as the normal and run contrary to our actual needs and long-term best interests. <u>We can in affect become our own worst enemy by perpetuating the influences in our lives which cause us to be irrational, diseased, restless, perennially dissatisfied, and unsure of our purpose and continually separated from our best interests.</u> How does this happen?

Many of us realize that we continue to make decisions that run contrary to our own best interests and yet we are seemingly powerless to affect long term change despite our best intentions and fervent resolution to be different. Many of us feel a lot like Sisyphus, the Greek character, who was condemned by the gods to continually roll a huge stone up a mountain only to have it roll back on us after we had painstakingly pushed it to the top. <u>We feel condemned to repeat the same awful patterns and purposeless actions over and over again without any hope of change</u>. What a panorama of hopelessness and futility it is! There is no mystery that so many in our culture are drugged to shield them from the pain of such an existence and that there are so many suffer from chronic depression and continually fight the thought of the false release of suicide.

There is a more excellent way but we must first understand the dynamics of these influences in our lives and the genesis of such a contrary and self-destructive behaviors.

It all starts in our family of origin in fact the modern way of grouping all these influences in an individual's life is under the banner of "Family of Origin Issues." Basically, it means if you are alive you are going to have issues.

There is no perfect family Petrie dish. Everyone has an equal opportunity to be messed up, but some have suffered such devastating early childhood experiences that it seems they are given a mandate to fail in every area of their lives. What sort of influences are we talking about here? Some experts refer to Type A traumas and Type B traumas.

Type A traumas are those events that actually happened in a person's life: for example; physical, emotional, and sexual abuse. That kind of early experience will color every aspect of an individual's sense of self- worth and personal value. These kinds of trauma color the most basic idea of the self and destroy any sense of protection and safety that a child must have to develop and thrive.

That environment in early childhood imparts a very real sense that the world is unsafe and intentionally hurtful. Even more damaging is that is teaches that child that there is something fundamentally wrong with them; that they are flawed and unlovable. That is the genesis of the Shame we will address more completely in another part of this book. The person who is subjected to these harsh and terrible influences early in life will be given a lens to see the world which will always make life in general an unsafe and painful experience.

That is the definition of stress. But sadder still is the belief system that develops from those experiences that says this is all they deserve. And to prove that they will continually place themselves in situations that will perpetuate their idea of themselves as broken, flawed, and unlovable. In effect, giving them an appetite for the very influences that wounded them in the first place.

The trouble is that so many of these things happen when we are too young to be able to sort them out and even before we have language, so we are left with feelings but no understanding of how to control or even evaluate what is true or false.

These influences give us a false identity and we are not even aware that our true purpose and identity has been stolen from us. So, we continue to display the false identity believing that is who we are and ever will be. We will act out according to our sense of identity, good or bad and that will cause us to continually perpetuate the very influences that have wounded us in the first place; we become, in effect, our own jailor.

Type B traumas are more subtle. There is in each of us the desire to be safe, loved, accepted, affirmed, received, and encouraged; it is just an integral desire and longing of the human heart.

Now many of us never suffered verbal, sexual, and physical abuse but even still the longings of our hearts were still unsatisfied. Maybe because those individuals that had responsibility for us were unequipped, unaware, and unable to provide the emotional, spiritual, and affirming environment that is required for a child to thrive. Why? Perhaps they never received the nurturing they required and so they could not reproduce something they had never acquired, learned, or received themselves. Perhaps they were incapacitated by their own Type A abuse or impaired by alcohol, substance abuse or mental issues.

For whatever the reason Type B traumas count, but you can't put your finger on them as easily.

Chaos Eaters

You can't reference an event or a consequence of prolonged and continued exposure to abuse. But there is still an underlying, unsettled, tentative and cloying feeling that somehow everything is not right. That you are missing something essential to your wellbeing, but you can't articulate what is. Again, such a lack is hard to articulate; it is a feeling of not quite being up to standard of living with parts missing.

In Type B traumas it is the absence of certain fundamental things that is the issue; not the presence of things which can be documented and focused on. But the effects of these missing ingredients are equally devastating but also very frustrating because they are harder to discover and uncover. This, in effect, tends to cause a restlessness and insecurity which makes individuals very susceptible to false promises of completion and purpose. Their lack of confidence makes them susceptible to manipulation and control by individuals and false claims of quick fulfillment.

They desire to be filled but they are clueless about what they need. This too gives one an appetite for influences and experiences that run contrary to our own best interests. These traumas can also cause us to have an appetite for Chaos.

And another thing, chaos does not follow the rules; chaos so always outside the reach of rules and that is its power and attraction. Chaos promises a false sense of liberty and freedom; a way to announce your individuality and separation from all the rules and conformity. That promise is, of course a lie and a trap. Well-intentioned but ill-equipped people often step into the ring with Chaos, especially where loved ones are involved.

They think that their own sense of order and rightness will defeat the choice for Chaos in the lives of those they love. The truth that as long as Chaos is the choice of an individual, there is very little that you can do. And when you step into Chaos' ring you will be knocked on your butt more often than not. It is funny to me that I have many Christian friends that think they can "in Jesus Name" cause victory to come.

They put in their super Christian t-shirts and step in to the ring with Chaos and get their fannies handed to them, why? You can only defeat Chaos by remaining in the order of God. Step into Chaos's home court and you will generally get trounced, but if you stand in the order of God, Chaos will have no advantage over you.

On your home court you rule, because you choose order. It really is a matter of choice and unfortunately, we cannot choose for others. We get upset when bad choices wreak havoc in the lives of those we love. We talk to them about better choices but until their appetite for chaos is diminished, they will rebel against order and those who represent it.

I often think of the story of the prodigal son in the bible. It was obvious that the younger son had and appetite for chaos…" riotous living, "as it is called in the story.

It is interesting to me, that the father did not stop his son from making his choices or even lessen the consequences of those choices in his life. He didn't run after him to the pig pen.

Chaos Eaters

What he did do every though, was to look down the road for that erring and wayward son, hoping that the young man would come to himself; which he eventually did.

Think of what the prodigal's mother was saying to her seemingly dispassionate husband. Did she upbraid him as being insensitive and uncaring? Did the conversations go something like this?

"You never understood him. He was always more like me and if you loved me, really loved me, you would go after him. How can you just stand there and do nothing, he is OUR SON!"

Someday I think I will write a play about the prodigal son's mother; I think it would be funny and insightful. But there is a truth there that is often not spoken about the power of an individual to choose Chaos and how we should respond to it. Chaos will never response to the rules.

I am going to illustrate this point with a story about my two grandsons, Connor, and Dominik. They had a Wii game system, like everyone one else it seems, and they are able to compete in virtual version of a lot of sports, i.e. baseball, football, bowling and even boxing. I watched them when they were playing the Wii version of a boxing match one day.

Now Connor, the older boy, knew all the rules of the game and was playing accordingly. But Dominik, the younger brother didn't know the rules and he did not care about the rules. He just really wanted to punch his brother's virtual lights out in the game and WIN!

And he did win most of the time, which frustrated Connor to the limit of his very limited patience with his brother.

He kept explaining the rules to Dominik who simply ignored what Connor said, and punched his way through every round like a whirling dervish; Wii control flying and Connor complaining that he couldn't win because he didn't follow the rules! But win he did over and over again until Connor got tired of losing and switched the game to something, he had mastery over.

That is, it, folks! If you insist on taking your sorry game to Chaos ring you are going to get whooped; get smart and wait for the consequences of riotous living take its toll; THEN order has its opportunity. That is what happened with the Prodigal son. The vernacular today is "tuff love," and I think it is tougher on the ordered people than on the chaos-addicted, but the process must be patiently endured until an opportunity presents itself close to Orders home field advantage. Chaos is a defeated foe.

QUESTIONS

Where have you continued to make decisions that are contrary to your own best interest?

What are you doing to attempt to shield yourself from the pain of repeated poor decisions?

Chaos Eaters

What influences have caused you to develop a false identity?

Where do you need to exhibit "tuff love" with those around you?

CHAPTER THREE: PERSONALITY – STEPPING STONE OR STUMBLING BLOCK

"Why is the study of personality important? Simply put, each personality has a unique of strengths and weaknesses and a definite and singular perspective and set of preferences. Each of the four personality types process information, formulate responses and view life in a unique and particular way. To not understand those distinctions, we open ourselves up to a cornucopia of misunderstanding, miss information and conflict"
 Kathryn Murray

Over twenty years ago at the very beginnings of a ministry path, I owned a cabin and wanted to get a few friends together for a weekend, a very casual retreat; just time away and fellowship by the lake. There was a woman I knew at the time that had mentioned her interest in and study of archetypal personalities and I was intrigued. She told me that there were personality inventories available and suggested that it might be a good ice-breaker for the ladies I had invited to the cabin. I thought it would be a great conversation starter and a way for the group to get to know each other better.

I did not realize the information was going to structurally and formationally become the bedrock that I would minister from in the years ahead. It was just a "fun" thing to present.

As I know now, one of my dominant personality traits is sanguine, so I realize how important "fun" is to me, but more on that later. It may be hard to think now about how controversial a personality study was in church circles back then; psychology was very in tune with this theme, but psychology was still looked at with a lot of skepticism in those same circles.

I still have friends today who feel that study of that sort is, at its core, manipulative. I always say they are welcome to their opinion, but hardly anything that has been presented to me in my life made more sense than what I discovered in my study of personality. My understanding has affected every aspect of my interactions with people.

The information I have absorbed and taught over the years has its effect on my personal growth and understanding the distinct and varied and valid preferences of another's personality type has helped me accept the validity of viewpoints other than my own.

Without this understanding, what offsets the natural conflicts inherent in differing points of view? How do we address the real road blocks and impasses these misunderstandings cause in an individual's life, in families, work relationships and society as a whole? I have come to understand the importance of understanding personality for its short-term revelations and its long-term implications. I have presented these materials in the United States and internationally, and I am always amazed at how universal the constructs seem to be, and how helpful. I walk out on those platforms to minister and they hold in every situation, so I am convinced of their value and validity.

Chaos Eaters

There are a lot of materials available today on the study of personalities and many ways to describe the four basic personality types; business models usually assign letters to define the various models: D, I, S and C. Some materials use different animals to symbolize the personality types; Labrador, beaver, lion, and eagle. I am most familiar with Florence Littauer's materials, so I will use her methodology as I describe the four basic personality archetypes.

The words she uses go way back in history Hippocrates the Greek founder of modern medicine used them centuries ago to describe the various humors (predilections, traits; dare I say "personality" in each person): CHOLERIC indicated fire SANGUINE, blood, MELANCHOLY, water, and PLEGMATIC, bile.

As I introduce the characteristics of each of these personalities the way I would if you were in one of my seminars, I am sure you will find yourself relating to one or more of the archetypes. For many this will be a revelation because you have never really been given the opportunity to own-your God-given point of view or even have your point of view validated. Let me say at the outset; there is no BEST PERSONALITY type, even though some of you have often declared that the world would be a whole lot better if it was more like you! Let me also say that the study of personality can become just another way of marginalizing people and putting them in another box to be dismissed. To use the information in this way would run counter to the intent of the study.

First, the whole purpose of these studies has been to help me understand myself, and my preferences.

It has then allowed me to understand others' unique points of view, their preferences, and helped me APPRECIATE them.

Yes, that is right, we are talking about a real means to accept and grow from one another's DIFFERENCES! What a concept, and what an opportunity! This understanding has been such a gift to me in relationships, and I hope it is to you, too, because opposites attract, you need this information, but more about that later.

The first personality Type is the POWERFUL CHOLERIC.

You will never have to wonder about who is charge when a Choleric is in the house. They are made to give orders and lead situations. The Choleric is the natural leader and knows that they are the best suited and qualified to take charge that is in their DNA.

They expect loyalty and demand obedience; they are born confidant in their own abilities, born generals so to speak. I have a beloved Choleric in my life whose family declares that he is "a legend in his own mind" and so are all Choleric.

Cholerics are movers and shakers, the doers, and born leaders. We need people like that to take charge especially in difficult situations where a steady mind and a cool resolve are required. But with all that cool assurance and confidence do not expect a Choleric to second guess themselves; they are always convinced that they are right even when they are not and they view criticism as disloyalty.

They are not touchy-feely people what they exude in personal conviction they lack in compassion. They are not feeling people. They are thinkers and doers, and they are not very interested in how you feel about anything.

Don't look for the Cholerics to be warm and fuzzy people in your life, that is not in them. They will not require a lot of your input in their plan of action; they expect you to execute not formulate. A lot of them are management types

The standard predisposition of a Choleric is "My way or your stupid way!" Those who know someone like this, or live with them, you know it can be tough dealing with the Cholerics unflagging understanding of their correctness; translated, they are never wrong. You can grow old waiting for an apology from a Choleric that would mean they had to admit they were wrong a thing they are almost structurally and psychologically unfit to do.

Fortunately, the percentage of Cholerics in the culture is less than 11 percent as a rule. I say God is smart about that, it is fortunate that the sprinkling of this personality is limited in the population pool at large, but they are needed.

CHOLERICS NEED TO BE IN CONTROL

The second personality type is the PLAYFUL SANGUINE.

Everyone knows who the Sanguine is in their group. They are the" life of the party" people; they are loud and boisterous and always up for a good time. In fact, they are motivated by FUN.

They rebel against the dull and routine, get bored easily and always are looking for new admirers and audience for their stories and gaiety. Sanguines get strength from crowds and depend on the approval of others.

They will pout if they are not paid attention to and move from project to project when one ceases to be interesting – translated fun. The motto; "You only go around once, make sure you have a good time!" embodies them. They are a lot like children who never lose their sense of wonder and playfulness. They are great story tellers, entertainers, and the life of every group they enter.

Sanguines love people; after all, they make such a good audience. No one will greet you as warmly and forget as quickly as a Sanguine; they characteristically will have a hard time remembering names.

I am strongly Sanguine overshadowed by a strong Choleric. I have had to really work at remembering names and I am pretty good at it now but it took real effort on my part. I was often fond of saying, "that the only name I remembered in an introduction was my own!"

That is the way with Sanguines, every group interaction is an opportunity to perform and receive recognition and appreciation; the most important person in the room is always them. They know they flavor up any gathering with their wit and color and vivaciousness.

Sanguines cannot bear to think that anyone is not as delighted with them as they are in themselves. Because they are so dependent on the approval of the crowd they can easily get upset if they perceive that they are not received or appreciated.

They are thin-skinned often easily offended. But the Sanguines ill-humor is mostly short lived because it gets in the way of a good time and separates them for the crowd which they adore and need.

I believe Sanguines are really puzzled and hurt when they find out that some people think of them as grasping or too needy. They find it really hard to believe that anyone could think of them as anything but delightful. After all, they bring so much to the party; they are the fizz in the coke and the bubbles in the champagne.

Sanguines are also mostly a minority in the population, apparently too much of a good thing is often too much of a good thing.

SANGUINES NEED AN AUDIENCE.

The third type is the PERFECT MELANCHOLY personality.

A lot of times when people find out that they are strongly melancholy they resist that word because they think it implies that they are sad, and that is not the case at all. The melancholies embody the largest group of any of the four types in a population and there is a reason for that...THEY DO EVERYTHING.

Melancholies are the planners and implementers; they are list makers, appointment makers, schedule keepers and problem solvers. They figure out how to accomplish the tasks required in their families and in the communities, they belong to.

They make lists, set priorities and goals; they arrange the details and follow through when committed to a task.

Melancholies are not flighty, emotional, or hot-headed; they always have eyes on the goal and work tirelessly to accomplish the task at hand. The most important thing for them is the WORK; they are disciplined, reliable, loyal, efficient, tireless, and often overextended by the tasks assigned to them which they want to do PERFECTLY.

Their temperament makes them wary of change and distrustful of new things; they like the assurance of tradition and established ways of doing things. They make friends slowly and have many qualifiers they are naturally protective of their personal life and do not want anyone to know their business; so, they are slow to enter into relationships.

They are implementers and are more than a little skeptical of the unpredictable messiness of feelings. What do feelings have to do with anything anyway? To the Melancholy mind, it is what you do that counts and they are the doers.

Don't ask them what they feel about something. It is better to ask about what they are doing. Melancholies know what the other personalities must come to realize or risk peril to their plans and great schemes; THEY DO EVERYTHING, and are often NOT credited for all they are doing.

Although they would never say anything (you are supposed to know how hard they are working, and how important they are) they need TO BE APPRECIATED.

Failure to appreciate the efforts of a melancholy will have disastrous consequences.

They are not confrontational people; they do not get angry; they get even. They are also masters of passive-aggressive behavior. Let me explain, unlike other personalities, the melancholies have a steel trap for a memory; they don't forget anything…ANYTHING! I call them green stamp people.

Years ago, there were premium programs; chief among them was S&H Green stamps. It worked like this; participating retailers gave you green stamps with every purchase made which you collected in books. After the books were full you could take the completed books to the S&H Redemption store and get stuff.

The quiet unassuming worker-bee melancholy is like that. If you offend them, they will not confront you directly, that is not their style. No, you will get a green stamp placed in their book, complete with date and time of your offense, the weather that day, what you were wearing that day and whoever else was in the room. You are of course unaware that you have collected a green stamp and will continue to be until the day the book is full and redemption time has come.

Oh boy! Are you in for the surprise of your life; the quiet, compliant, hard-working melancholy is about to erupt like a Vesuvius, and all of those collected offenses are going to come spewing at you with dates, times, figures, exact phrases.

They will remember everything you have forgotten will spill all around you, and you are going to have a bad day in the home or office.

It is very difficult to recover from a full-blown Melancholy eruption because when the long suffering, patient, and hard-working melancholy blows there is hardly ever any going back. And all of this seems so atypical of the melancholy but they are deep people and long-suffering, and when they have had enough …they have had enough! People in leadership roles should understand that the success of their ideas and plans rest pretty squarely on the execution, drive, work-ethic, and perfection bias of all the melancholies in their group.

To not realize that and appreciate that is a common problem. Leaders, businesses, families, and churches can often alienate the worker bees in their pool and end up with great plans but no implementation.

When we are discussing the strength and weaknesses of the various personalities in a group setting, one thing I do is have the melancholy group stand up. They are generally the largest group in any group I survey.

Why do I have them stand up? I want the whole group to tell them one thing, "Thank you for all you do for us!" The melancholy reaction is almost always the same; first there is a kind of shock followed by a kind of false modesty and finally the satisfaction that recognition is long overdue and well deserved. Melancholies know how much they are doing and are glad that someone finally has the good sense to appreciate it.

MELANCHOLIES (THOUGH THEY WILL NEVER ADMIT IT OR ASK NEED) NEED APPRECIATION.

If you do not have the good sense to appreciate the melancholies in your life you will pay for it and so will your relationships, your family, your business, and your great plans; word to the wise. Remember, they do everything and remember everything!

The fourth personality type is the PEACEFUL PLEGMATIC.

This personality is the opposite of the outgoing attention seeking Sanguine. The last place they want to be is in the front of any group.

Phlegmatic are not performers; they are observers and love to be in the background doing their job without drama, living a quiet life in a peaceful environment. I often think of them as the glue which holds society because they do seek to impose their opinion on any one.

They are great listeners, in a world that increasingly listens to nothing but its own point of view. It is refreshing to encounter non- polarizing individuals who will give you audience without judgment or opinion. Phlegmatic do that.

Surprisingly, the quite unassuming phlegmatic also possesses a killer sense of humor. Unlike the Sanguine who are natural humorists and story tellers and constantly want to please the audience. Phlegmatic humor is observational.

Since they have no desire to be the center of attention, they sit back and watch everyone else make fools of themselves. They don't miss much and when their humor surfaces it is likely to be a "perfect zinger" direct, to the point and stunningly accurate and funny. People scratch their heads at such times and marvel where that all came from since the peaceful phlegmatic is so quiet most of the time.

Phlegmatic are quiet and unassuming but to consider that weakness would be a big mistake; phlegmatics have an iron will which is not easily deterred. Phlegmatic hate conflict and will avoid it like the plague; anger, rage and hostility really scare them. They will always seek a peaceful resolution to a situation. So, what might be construed as capitulation and agreement in the mind of the more forceful personality types when they interact with them is in actuality just long-suffering and self – preservation.

Phlegmatics in my audiences always smile knowingly when I reveal one of their secrets; they have a built-in safe house in their psyche. It works like this; if phlegmatic are being pressured and pressed upon by those who do not understand them, they will simply seem to agree and then retreat to this "other place" that they have within them.

They just go there with a smile on their face where they wait until the bad person or situation goes away. When offending parties vacate the scene (no doubt thinking they have won the quite unassuming phlegmatic over to their point of view) they come back to their now peaceful world and DOES EXACTLY WHAT THEY WANT TO DO.

Chaos Eaters

I can speak personally about my education with regard to a phlegmatic s unique sensitivity. I am as defined in every personality inventory that I have taken as a Choleric/Sanguine.

I have mentioned that for most of us an inventory will reveal a bias toward two of the four archetypes. As is often the case, those closest to you are often the exact opposite of your personality types, hence; opposites attract but there are underlying inherent conflicts in personal preferences and world view. I and my daughter are no exception.

Melissa is as opposite from me personality wise as it is possible to be and to add to those differences; Melissa is also adopted so we do not share any family DNA or family traits.

Back when I was in college, I remember that there was a great debate in my psychology classes of the relative importance of nature (blood line, shared DNA, etc.) and nurture (education, social imprinting, etc.). Back then, since I knew everything, and was not a parent, I was definitely in the in the *nurture* camp. I really thought that education and child rearing and positive societal influences would trump nature every time.

I was wrong, and my journey with my daughter over the last thirty plus years has been a real eye-opener and education for me.

Being a Sanguine I consider myself a great communicator. And because I am also a Choleric, I am often convinced that I am right about most things. (It is the nature of the beast as I have explained).

My dilemma is always how to be communicate my "rightness," and still have my audience like me, some of you are smiling as you read this because you know it can be a real tight wire act. I also love words, and believe that God never made us so much like Him as when He gave us the ability to speak. Because of that perspective I have a bias; I think that words when properly communicated will change anything. I am wrong in that too, as my journey with Melissa has clearly taught me. In our formative years,

I always felt that my strong forthright (manipulative and aggressive, if truth be told) dealings with my daughter were very affective. Until I realized that what I was saying or doing was having very little affect. I foolishly believed my bullying and pontificating had worked in an agreement, because of quietness on Melissa's part. I thought I had won. Silly me, as I came to realize later, she was agreeing just to get me out of her face while she retreated to the "safe place" every Phlegmatic has until the "bad person," (me) went away.

The frustrating thing was after I felt I had achieved agreement and a commitment from her for changed behavior, she did exactly what she wanted to do! She was behaving like the famous iron will of phlegmatic that I referred to earlier.

So why is all this important? Simply put, each personality has a unique set of strengths and weaknesses, and a definite perspective and preference. So, if we fail to understand how each of these personalities process information, formulate responses, and view life we open ourselves to a cornucopia of misunderstanding, misinformation, and conflict.

Any group will reflect the distribution of these personality archetypes within its membership, starting within families. Have you noticed that a shared DNA does not produce a homogenized product? Each family member is going to be different, sometimes dynamically and dramatically so. I see it in my own family of origin.

My sisters and I do have certain physical and natural characteristics and share a definite family history, but we are totally different individuals. And we each have a way of dealing with the basic issues of life; relationships, conflict management and our expectation of what is acceptable and not acceptable. We all have different comfort zones and they are not congruent. There lies the opportunity for conflict, dissension, offense, bitterness, and the whole raft of ills that all relationships are subject to.

We have learned over the years, because we have chosen to stay in touch and work through a lot of issues. We have learned together and individually how to" let sleeping dogs lie" so to speak. We are not often seeking conflict with each other these days; there was a time when that was true, but conflict invariably comes.

The beauty of long-term relationships like ours which now span sixty years is that we have a track record and a solid core of experience that keeps us connected as a group – even when one or more of us are disconnected. Now, when one or more of us is out of sorts with the others, there is a synergy of the whole that keeps us connected. We have *consciously* chosen that sustained connection.

After our mother died, we found ourselves at a crossroads, but committed to each other at that time to remain a family.

That commitment has been sorely tested over the years. It has often been strained and frayed, but it remains. That is not always true across the population. I meet so many people who have very little to do with siblings and very little good to say about their family members as well.

I think disassociation is one of the great tragedies of our modern life. We are so disconnected from some very basic needs; among them the need to belong, to be accepted, and to have a special place that no one else can fill. Sadly, too many people walk around without that basic anchor which was so common just a few decades ago. Many of us live in a dis-associated and random state, without roots or community which are so vital to creating a defining platform on which to build a confident life, that all adds to the chaos that is so prevalent these days.

Do the personal preferences and personality traits of my sisters affect our ongoing relationships? In every way! In our family pool, three of us have a lot of strong Choleric tendencies which leads to many interesting dynamics. Remember, Cholerics are always right – even when they are not.

Thankfully we are all tempered by other personality traits; remember we are usually a combination of two dominant archetypes. I, for example, am a Choleric /Sanguine so I want to be right but I also want to be accepted and liked; that often translates into "I want you to do as I say," but I also want you to like me while you are doing it. Another in the same family pool is a Choleric/Melancholy, who not only wants you to do what they say, they demand that you do it perfectly because they know what perfect is.

Fortunately, God gave our particular family a gift; we have one person who is exhibits among many other things a strong desire for peace; that is the strengths of the Phlegmatic personality. That individual is always in contact with all three of the other members of our little group. If you want to know what is happening with the other sisters, she usually knows, and she will strive to keep the bonds of peace between us all, which is no easy task. She has no "skin in the game" so to speak and it allows all of us breathing space. Her role in the family is essential. As I said, the peace-loving phlegmatic is glue which holds society together, and I see that clearly in my own family member.

The more I realize the dynamics involved, I can avoid getting stuck in my own sense of "rightness." And, the more I understand about preferences, the more educated my interaction has become with my sisters, and in my relationships at large.

It is interesting to me that as I look back on my formative years, my father had his own unique demons and challenges; his alcoholism was a defining fact of our childhood and young adult years. His suicide in 1971 was a pivotal moment in all our lives. Still, he also had a kind of primitive understanding of the differences in each of his girls. He wasn't home a lot while we were growing up, but I know that he didn't treat any us the same way.

I have already said, I had a particular place as the first born, but he recognized the uniqueness in each of us. Sadly, his addiction issues didn't allow for much of an expansion of his rudimentary understanding, but he clearly had it.

Each of his girls were unique, and to his credit he always told us we could do anything we wanted to do. He had a favorite story that came from his love for the railroad, called the "Little Train That Could." My sisters and I still say that familiar refrain "I think I can …I think I can," today. And you know what, as the years have passed and the decades have piled up, WE COULD.

That belief has been an enduring legacy. Each of us have achieved and preserved and succeeded in our individual lives. My mother loved us all. We all realized that, but she had her favorite – her baby. We all understood it, but we knew she loved us, and that was incredibly powerful in our dysfunctional home. Many today in similar circumstances could not say the same, and the lovelessness contributes to the estrangement that many feel ever day of their lives.

I believe a basic understanding of the temperaments contributes to important society building components such as child rearing. I cannot tell you how many times a person first exposed to the personality inventory will have a real paradigm shift when they recognize how different they were from their parents and siblings. Up until that point those differences were a source of alienation, confusion, and sometimes rejection and shame.

Think of the possible combinations in any family tree. For example, what are the long-term effects if you are a peace loving phlegmatic with a Choleric parent, in your face all the time telling you to shape up and measure up. What about a fun loving Sanguine dropped into a largely melancholy work-first-fun-later family?

Chaos Eaters

That is where the jokes about the milkman father come from. In every family there are misfits who seem incongruent to the family pattern, and are made to feel they do not belong. Just imagine the silent observer in a family of performers, the bossy little guy in a family of melancholies, or the busy little organizer in a family of Sanguines or Phlegmatics.

Note too, that cultures have these same personality markers too. My Mid-west town is populated by Northern Europeans; Germans and Norwegians and Netherlanders…the most common name in the phone book is Anderson and Johnson. The northern Europeans are a great many things; industrious, law abiding, reserved as a rule, quiet in a group and like to and respectable and a bit apprehensive about change…in a word a population that is largely Melancholy.

My family always embraces the Irish side of our family tree, even though we are actually just as Swedish as we Irish. We are a loud party, decidedly Sanguine in our outlook. We always think we are the best thing that ever happened to the party, even when others may not agree. We have been told to cut the enthusiasm and noise too many times to count.

Once, I was awaiting my friend at an event held at a Norwegian/Lutheran college in town. As I waited, I took notice of the quiet, patient, largely Norwegian people coming to the event. Many of them were wearing distinctive blue and white patterned sweaters, with silver buttons brought back from their trips to Norway, the old country.

Watching that parade, I realized why I had always felt eccentric to the community; they were Norwegian and I was Irish. That conflict is reflected even in the literature of the early settlement of this area. Go read Karl Rolvaag to see what I mean.

It was a real eye-opener for me and a platform for my further investigations into the cultural and personal differences inherit in personality archetypes. Understanding the differences goes a long way to allowing us to embrace the similarities, and grow as families, communities, and nations. Not factoring in these inherent preferences increasingly contributes to an atmosphere of alienation and misunderstanding in individuals, communities, and nations.

For real understanding we must always attempt to see the lens that others see the world through. For many, that is a staggering revelation, because we often think our own personal preferences and opinions are the standard. In my teaching opportunities I frequently do an exercise to illustrate this point. I find any number of glass-wearing participants, and ask them to exchange glasses.

The result is telling and comical; what is perfect and tailor-made for one individual is absolutely useless for someone else. And that is the human condition; just as it is very difficult to see through another person's lens prescription, it is extremely difficult to factor in another person's preferences and points of view. But if relationships individually and in society as a whole are to prosper and grow in these matters; we must take these factors into consideration.

I cannot end this discussion of personality without addressing what I like to call OPPOSITIONAL ATTRACTION. I phrase it that way because I think it more honestly describes the mechanics of partner formation. The phrase comes from the adage "opposites attract." I absolutely feel this is true. I believe there is in each of us a hope to be a part of a "completer set" and intrinsically we are drawn to partners who have qualities different than our own.

We are drawn to those who are different from ourselves. But there is another adage I like to quote which is just as true, "the grass is greener on the other side of the fence (but it usually needs cutting!)" Looking at the personalities and the preferences inherent in the way they view the world, you can begin to see how this would play out.

The CHOLERIC, who is always right, and always must be in control, would naturally find themselves attracted to the peaceful PLEGMATIC who never has an agenda accept to keep the peace and get along. CHOLERICS need people in their lives who want to make peace because peace is not their nature. The problem is, after a while the CHOLERIC can tire of always being charge, and may begin to push the PLEGMATIC to do more, and not be so passive.

Well, when the CHOLERIC roars, the PLEGMATIC retreats into their safe place. And so, the conflict begins...get out the lawn mower!

What about the work obsessed MELANCHOLY?

What could be more attractive that the lively fun SANGUINE, all sparkly and full of life? A Melancholy partner is a great contrast and an opposite to their workaholic propensity. But after the honey moon period is other the MELANCHOLY may be tempted to "fix" their lovely mate, and make them more serious and work oriented. That only serves to make the sensitive SANGUINE feel rejected and misunderstood. When the SANGUINE is not having fun, they are like a fish out of water. Fun is their natural environment, and since the MELANCHOLY is naturally suspicious of fun as the enemy of getting things done.... hedge clipper please, we have some work to do here!

I have a cousin who is absolutely the most SANGUINE personality I have ever known. Her partner in life was one of the MELANCHOLY men I have ever met and German! They were a classic paring of opposites; but as he so often said he knew intrinsically that if he married someone like himself, he would never have any fun. He knew that my lively cousin was exactly the spice he needed in his life. the secret to their life together was that he genuinely enjoyed what she brought to his life and did not try to change her ...Much!

He recognized it would be unkind to her, and detrimental to his own quality of life. One of the last things he said to her in his life was," Do you know how much you please me?" Doesn't that speak volumes? There were a lot of things he could have focused on or tried to change in my cousin, but he decided to embrace the differences in his wife and it made all the difference.

Chaos Eaters

One of the problems in our throw away culture is that relationships are increasingly disposable. After the blush of the romantic when there are hormones and expectations and everyone feels that their partner is "just like me!" Generally, not the truth and about two years into the relationship; they begin to say things like "You're not the man or woman I married!" Of course, they aren't! I believe that most people marry the reflection of themselves they see in their partner. A few years in, they begin to see the real person beyond the mirror of their hopes, needs, expectations, and completer mythology.

Then, look out… get the lawnmower!

In reality, there is some grass that needs clipping. Look at the divorce statistics these days. Years ago, it was the "seven-year itch" that collapsed marriages. ow that period has shrunk dramatically to two years or less. The instant gratification, disposable culture leaves brokenness in its wake. Sadly, children of these relationships inherit a tsunami of rejection and insecurity in the wake of the dissolution of these relationships.

I hear so many young girls talking about "Baby daddy drama." There are increasingly more and more children born into single parent households. A generation is being children born to shaky foundations which quake in the early stage of their lives leaving them felling abandoned and the subject of tension and argumentation. What a foundation for an appetite for CHAOS.

QUESTIONS

Which one of the personality types most sounds like your personality?

How has your personality conflicted or meshed with those in your family or in friendships?

How does understanding personality types change (or not change) how you will interact with others going forward?

CHAPTER FOUR: SHAME – THE PETRIE DISH OF DYSFUNCTION

"There is so much confusion and misunderstanding about SHAME'S power to cripple and stunt emotional and spiritual growth in our lives. It starts with an inappropriate grasp of the meaning of the word itself... SHAME is mistakenly used in the same context and supposedly with the same meaning as GUILT. The two words are not interchangeable and understanding that principle is essential to grappling the devious, shape –changing nature of the power of SHAME in our lives."
Kathryn Murray

There are few conditions that can produce an appetite for CHAOS as a constant acid bath of SHAME in an individual's life.

There is so much confusion and misunderstanding about SHAME'S power to cripple and stunt emotional and spiritual growth in our lives. It starts with an inappropriate grasp of the meaning of the word itself; SHAME is mistakenly used in the same context and supposedly the same meaning as GUILT. The two words are not interchangeable and understanding that principle is essential to understanding the devious, shape-changing nature of the power of SHAME in our lives.

So, I am going to take time to present how I have come to understand the critical differences between SHAME and GUILT.

First, understand, I believe that GUILT is a fully activated part of our conscience which acts as a critical evaluator of our actions. It serves as a moral barometer of what we see as right or wrong.

The important thing to remember is that GUILT is paired with our actions…we have to have done something wrong to activate a feeling of GUILT. GUILT in its pure essence and intention is a help to us; it serves as a moral compass and helps us evaluate actions within our framework of our moral code.

Now I believe that as the North Star is to a sense of direction, GUILT is God- given and its purpose is to keep us on course. It is intentionally in our psychic DNA and is intended to reveal the order of God in all things. I am not talking about a manipulative application of guilt used to control others. This is what most of think when the word GUILT is mentioned.

Guilt in its purest state is intended to lead us to right actions. It is a warning device that lets us know let us know when we have violated our interior sense of right and wrong. In introducing the concept of an absolute right and wrong sensitivity within our very nature I realize that I invite derision and mockery. This is day of moral relativity rooted in the belief that there is no real right or wrong and no way to judge our own or other's actions.

Obviously, I don't believe that; I see GUILT as a God-given teacher which is designed to help us do the right thing and draw us closer to a righteous, loving Creator.

To feel GUILT, you must have done something your internal sense of morality declares wrong. YOU HAVE DONE SOMETHING wrong and feel guilty about it. I believe it is an opportunity to take a second look at our actions and make them right. Now, we can walk past the guilt and continue to ignore the teacher within us. We often do with sad and long-lasting effects.

In fact, I believe when continually we walk past the counsel of guilt in our lives, we begin to lose our sensitivity to what is right and dull the effectiveness of Guilt in our lives. There is real confusion in. But to intentionally overstate the point; when you feel GUILTY there is always an opportunity to evaluate of your actions. When we have violated your conscience, GUILT is asking for re-evaluation of your motivations. This may seem strange to say, but GUILT in is essence is a good thing.

SHAME on the other hand has nothing to commend itself; it is a destroyer. Its very nature is a lie. SHAME'S purpose is to erode and abort the core essence of the individual's sense of who they are and thwart an understanding of their importance and destiny.

I am convinced SHAME is a spirit which loses is grasp and destructive power as its nature is revealed and its purpose called out and challenged. SHAME masks itself in many ways and hides in blind spots and dark alleys in our minds. SHAME is rooted in experience.

Over the years, I have found the genesis of a shame-based personality is often experiences of early childhood.

Often in the pre-verbal years when the child's sense of self is just developing and totally dependent on the world around it, Shame enters in to promote a false sense of self and achieve its purpose of distorting identity formation.

Shame is always feeling based. I say the seed for a shame-centric life is often planted in a child's early experiences within the home. If a child is nurtured and taken care of physically, emotionally, and spiritually there is a message sent to the child's core sense of who they are. I am important. I am taken care of. I am safe and secure, and most importantly, I am lovable.

On the contrary, if a child's home environment is chaotic, careless, and even hostile the message received is just the opposite; life is not safe. I am not secure. I am not taken care of and most importantly, I am not lovable. All these early life experiences create the basic sense of who the child is in the world. And depending on whether a child is received and celebrated or resented and merely tolerated; all these early interactions in the primary home environment set a pattern for their thoughts about their place in the world.

Most of these learned patterns must be verbalized because the child is too young for language. But ALL these first experiences will result in feelings either positive or negative and those feelings have very powerful and long-lasting consequences. Those primary feelings never go away; they are part of the first markers in the child's brain and spirit and soul.

Those feelings form the basis of a world view and their own sense of empowerment and self-worth.

Chaos Eaters

I have found most of the people who have shame, rage, abandonment, or rejection issues are totally unable to verbalize those words at the beginning of their recovery. They have lived with these feelings so long they assume they are a part of who they are... they are in fact broken, rejected, unlovable and abandoned. Those feelings are just as much a part of their emotional personality as the DNA is in their physical person.

What is the message to child when the adults in their world are careless or even cruel and abusive? In their world, THEY are the big people, the POWER people and the child is small, powerless, and dependent. If the BIG PEOPLE in their first world are destructive and harmful what is the message the child receives?

It is the basic massage of SHAME; you are not lovable. You are broken. You are bad because if you weren't BAD the big people would take better care of you. It is your fault they treat you this way. It is all you deserve. In fact, that is often the language of the abuser to their victims when making then feel worthless, powerless, and rejected is the purpose in such situations.

Wouldn't it be something if the abused baby could sit up and tell their abusers "HEY! Do you know that I am the child here and you are making me feel rejected and unlovable? You are the BIG PEOPLE and you should know better. Don't you realize you are making me feel badly about myself. I am going to have a lot of problems in my life because you are failing to do your job!"

Wouldn't you love to see that dialog?

In terms of recovery someone has to introduce the abused, neglected and rejected child in the adult to the LANGUAGE OF RECOVERY. The feelings are tamed by the vocabulary of understanding. People think often they can lock all the bad stuff of their childhood in a dark closet with a double lock and throw away the key.

Denial is the path of least resistance and they attempt to build a life on a faulty foundation. But such a foundation is hardly ever secure; there is just too much in the closet that is demanding and noisy. The feelings we are trying to forget and ignore come out sideways and with embarrassing intensity.

We pretend we do not know why we are so angry, isolated, or insecure; that is just the way we are, PERIOD! We tell others to accept it or hit the road. We form relationships out of our brokenness because we do not feel worthy of good things in our lives. We never really share ourselves with others because we fear intimacy and the revelation that true relationships bring. We are afraid of exposure. I call it the "glass underwear experience" who wants that sort of scrutiny when you feel that deep down you are flawed and unlovable.

That is the basic voice of SHAME in an individual's life. "If people really get to know you, they will know what you know; that you are broken and worthless! Don't let anyone in. Keep your guard up and perform because if they know what you really are, they will reject you." The other lie about SHAME is that it always says," You are the only one who feels this way. In the whole history of the world, YOU ALONE are the biggest piece of worthless garbage.

And you are alone and cannot be reconciled because of your brokenness."

I have said before, this is one of my favorite moments in my ministry when I am addressing the lies of SHAME. Why? Because when I ask the audience who has ever felt this way almost all the hands in the audience go up. So, I invite everyone to look around and see the upraised hands.

What a moment when an individual can see how much of a lie they have believed and how much company they have on that bus. The moment the lie begins to be revealed is the very moment you can begin the empowerment process. Why? Because you have a name for that feeling you have allowed to define you all your life.

When you can name SHAME, you begin to defeat it.

The power of recovered language begins to neutralize the lie of the feelings. When people get a hold of the word SHAME in relation to their feelings, the tyrant's reign is weakened. The power of that stronghold rooted in the feeling of SHAME is over.

Recognition and reconciliation are now possible as the stronghold loses its authority in a life. It is a process of course, but people can learn not to accommodate those feelings every time they chose to call. When the lie and the feelings attached to the lie comes again, they can be equipped to call SHAME it out and recognize it for the lie that it is. Slowly they will begin to know the voice of SHAME is not their voice or their truth. That is powerful reconciliation and remedy, an effective weapon and tool for recovering from the poisonous effect of SHAME in a life.

To summarize; SHAME is feeling based understanding of who you are based largely as the result of things done to you without your permission. Its purpose is to keep you bound in your understanding, and make you feel, at your core, that you are broken and unlovable. SHAME generally has its genesis in our life in our early life experiences.

Things are said and done to us without our permission or consent in such a way as to make us feel a false responsibility for other people's actions.

As a child you were put in situations where you are made to feel as if you gave consent to totally inappropriate and out of your control actions. The truth is you are not responsible for those actions because you did not choose to have those things done to you, on you or around you. To believe you somehow brought those things on yourself because you weren't good enough is a lie.

You did not choose to do these things; they were done to you. You are not responsible for these actions or the feelings that resulted from these experiences. It is not your weight to carry. Understanding this concept is the beginning of the end of the power of SHAME to shape and control your life.

There is a tyranny of feelings in the pre-verbal world. We have experiences which create feelings even when we do not have words to communicate the effects of those feelings.

Recovery begins when we begin to get a language to explain the landscape of our souls. We can use language [WORDS] to tame the "feeling-beasts" within us.

The process of attaining a vocabulary of recovery gives a platform for continued victory over the closeted and secretive demons in our inner landscape.

To attain this vocabulary is an essential part of recovery, new life, and victory over the CHAOS of unexamined, persistent feelings.

QUESTIONS

Name something you feel guilty for. Now, answer this question: "Is this something I have actually done, that I SHOULD feel guilty for?"

Where have you kept your guard up to keep others from getting to know who you really are? What would the result be if you let them in?

What are one or two experiences that have caused you to feel SHAME. Since words are the key to taming the "feeling-beasts," make a commitment to tell at least one person your story.

CHAPTER FIVE: THE INTRA-PERSONAL DYNAMICS OF SHAME

"SHAME is an inner dialog which always loops a message that an individual is innately broken, flawed and unlovable. Because the tape is constantly playing, the SHAME-based individual lives in constant fear of exposure. There a false identity constantly producing a hyper-vigilance that seeks to shelter and cover up the wounded and broken notion of themselves from being exposed in relationships"
 Kathryn Murray

Although I have addressed Shame in another section of this book, I want to underline some of the basic relational aspects of shame, and the shame based individual here.

Shame is the inner dialog which always loops a message saying the individual is innately broken, flawed, and unlovable. Because the tape is constantly playing, the shame based individual lives in constant fear of exposure. They present themselves in ways that constantly monitor the reaction of people they are in contact with. Many become emotional chameleons adapting to every situation in a way that keeps their inner sense of worthlessness deeply hidden.

This false identity is constantly producing in us a sense of hyperawareness that seeks to shelter the wounded, and a broken notion of themselves from being exposed.

That exposure is what I call the "glass underwear experience." It is scalding and painful because we think it exposes us. So, if a Shame-based individual lives in a continual state of fearing exposure, imagine the challenge the prospect of a deep, personal relationship presents.

Deep, intimate relationships by their nature require openness and shared emotional typography. If one or more of the individuals suffer from a shame-based fear of exposure there will be a lot of posturing and performance seeking approval; still there will be a lack of true intimacy that requires opening to one another and is the heart of true friendship and relationship.

Something will always be missing because one or both of the individuals see themselves as having missing pieces; a brokenness which they feel exposing would ruin any chance of continuing the relationship. The opposite is true we know it, but the fear of exposure is the root cause of many problems in relationships; a deep-seated fear that to really expose oneself would cause irreparable loss and rejection.

The relational dynamics of friendship are tricky for a shame-based person. I explain it this way; usually I have two ill-drawn (art not being my gifting) stick figures on a bridge walking toward each other. Both of them have their arms extended to each other and seem to be approaching each other with equal enthusiasm, a smile on each of their stick figure faces, so to speak. But throw conflict into this scenario, which is inevitable and part of the dynamic of any relationship and the shame-based person will ALWAYS

TAKE ALL THE BLAME FOR THE CONFLICT.

Picture one of them falling off a draw bridge that has opened up and thrown them into their own personal whirlpool of self-doubt, incrimination, self-absorption, and criticism. That is the SHAME SPIRAL. Shame-based individuals will blame themselves for every aspect of the relationship breakdown. It doesn't even enter their consciousness that the other party involved was a participant in the breakdown. More importantly, the shame-based individual would never, ever believe the other party has any responsibility for the breakdown. They will blame themselves for everything that has happened.

It is a place of total self-scrutiny and self-loathing; a totally inward focused state of mind. The dialog in their heads will likely say, "Well I should have known this would happen between us; now they know what I have known all along. I am broken and unlovable. Often, they will ask why they ever thought they could be different. They will say things like, "I am not worthy to be loved."

The SHAME-SPIRIAL is a slippery slope and since it attempts to cancel out ALL outside influences, the effect of a shame spiral incident can last a long time. For some people that raw, exposed, and vulnerable feeling is their daily bread; they have come to believe they will always feel the same. They have no hope that anything will ever change, and feel the inner flawed part of them must always be covered up and protected from exposure. Shame-based individuals believe no one could see their brokenness and still love them. To expose themselves would result in their always being alone, rejected, and unlovable. The SHAME SPIRAL is a lonely place. I think of it as an emotional grave.

The other aspect of the shame-based identity is the voice in your head declaring a lie which is this: "YOU ARE THE ONLY ONE WHO FEELS THIS WAY AND EVERYONE ELSE IN THE WHOLE WORLD IS OKAY."

Know that we are not dealing with rational constructs here, but rather with bed-rock emotional underpinnings that have not been exposed to the light of reason or identity. On paper those ideas are patently ridiculous, but shame is not a rational influence in our lives.

Shame is emotion-based and feels real, but is not necessarily true. It is always a highlight to me in ministry situations when I expose this lie to the audience. When I ask if they have felt the way I have described, almost every hand in the audience goes up. It is a powerful moment when I have them look around and see all of those who have believed they were the only one to ever feel this way.

The number of hands raised around the audience is a reality check for everyone. For many, that moment may be the first time the concept has been confronted and exposed as false. That moment is always one of the high points of my presentation. I LOVE EXPOSING THE LIES INHERENT IN SHAME. They are so subtle and submerged in practice, but so patently false when the light of truth uncovers them. That lie embedded deep in the soul is a fundamental lens by which the shame-based person views the world.

I came to knowledge of these things in a very personal way. It was a family gathering at my sister's house in Sioux City, Iowa. It was warm enough evening for people to be outside in the back yard of her home.

Chaos Eaters

I remember the moment very clearly. I was using the bathroom and looked out the window to a panorama of mostly my family and it hit me, "They (it is always a they) ARE ALL OKAY, AND

I AM NOT!" I am different, broken, and not like them at all. AND, I AM THE ONLY ONE OF THEM WHO FEELS THIS WAY.

I am an outcast even among my own family." I remember sitting, completely emotionally shut down in my sister's living room. I simply was no longer able to join in the gathering (SHAME SPIRIAL) and yet unable to gather myself to leave.

I was stuck. Periodically, someone or other would notice my absence and come in looking for me, but the paradox of these situations is even though you desperately need someone to enter your emotional space, you are equally desperate to keep them out for fear of exposure and rejection. It was like that for me. I stayed at the gathering, not involved but physically present; appearances matter right? But when everyone had retired for the evening, I retrieved my sleeping daughter from the upstairs bedroom where she had been sleeping, and got in my car heading home to Sioux Falls, SD.

I was crying the whole way home, just undone emotionally and desperate. I knew this feeling was not an isolated incident. I realized with a kind of dread that I felt this exposed and isolated a lot, and the awareness was depressing.

I was desperate for understanding, and the next morning a friend called with the number of a local counselor.

Now it came seemingly "out of the blue," so to speak, but I was desperate enough to make an appointment.

So, I began my journey out of Shame.

Through that counselor I was finally able to examine my life in a safe place. I began to realize my feelings of impotence over my father's alcoholism made me feel responsible for his behavior. And since his behavior didn't change, I felt like a failure.

Now of course, child-me had no power to change my father's behaviors. I know that now. I probably knew on some intellectual level before I began counseling. But the emotional heart of me that was still locked in silence and anger and self-loathing.

Those feelings were misdirected. I did not blame anyone but myself. I know now this is the way of dysfunctional relationships. Children see the actions of the BIG PEOPLE, but when things go terribly wrong in ways they are not equipped to understand; they blame themselves. They begin to think things would be different if they were different. And when things do not change, they blame themselves.

The genesis of that voice is that it repeats repeatedly, "You are broken. You are unlovable. You are a failure."

Though the counseling I was able to connect with my feelings of anger towards my father. It was liberating. It was necessary. It was overdue, but it wasn't the conclusion of the process. I know a lot of people who enter the counseling process and get stuck in the anger.

Chaos Eaters

If you remain there, you place yourself in the role of a victim. That isn't enough to break the cycle of SHAME. I remember the day of the "long session" I had dreaded it. The counselor had been preparing me for the long session for weeks.

The thought of it scared me and the day it was finally scheduled, I really wanted to be sick. I came into the session very anxious and defensive. I was angry at the counselor for putting in this situation. I was anger at myself for agreeing to come. I was an emotional wreck, and remember being curled up in a ball on the couch for quite a while just wailing.

It was like some emotional geyser inside of me blew. It was alternately terrifying and strangely cathartic. And then, it was like my father actually came into the room and I let him have it. I cursed him for his drinking. I cursed him for having to carry the weight of his alcoholism as if it were my problem.

I cursed him for killing himself, and leaving all of us to again pick up the pieces for his disastrous choices. I cursed him for the fact that I was always choosing bright, broken guys to fix. It was a long session.

At the end of it there was a real lightness and an emotional opening that I had never experienced before. It was then I realized that with all his issues, and all the issues I had inherited from his addiction, I loved him. I didn't love him for the way I wanted him to be. I loved him for who he was and I forgave him. I forgave him and accepted his choices were his own and that I could be free.

It was the beginning of a language of recovery for me. I began to understand the voice of Shame and the lies it tells in a life. I began to walk out of situations that used to throw me into a shame-spiral.

I finally understood I was only responsible for my actions in any given situation. I was able to begin to break the code and discover and love myself. I was able to stop trying to be what people wanted and expected me to be and be myself.

Shame based people are always hiding behind a mask, and that is *so* exhausting. They end up trying to give people what they want, so they do not see the fear of exposure in you. As I gave myself permission to be who I was,

I found relationships based on the real me. What a liberation that is! The beginning steps of that journey were so many years ago, I can say the shame-spiral is still an occasional event in my life – but it is very rare.

I have the tools to defeat it. I hope this is encouragement to you. For some of you, shame and its lies are your daily bread, and so I give you my testimony as a reason to hope for a clearer future.

QUESTIONS

Shame-based individual live in constant fear of exposure. How has fear of exposure impacted your life? Your relationships?

The shame-based person will often take all the blame in a conflict. When have you allowed yourself to take blame when you were clearly not the cause?

When have you felt you were only one who feels this broken, alone, shameful, and unworthy?

CHAPTER SIX: SHAME, FEAR, AND CONTROL

All of that is a part of the instant nature of our culture at present. If we want it; we want it now. We even want our emotional and spiritual issues fast-tracked and easily packaged; easy to access and easy to digest. Now, anyone who has ever done any serious rehabilitation and restoration work knows that just isn't how it works. Personal growth is jagged and often slow and there is much fear to overcome in the process of excavating an authentic self...AND IT AIN'T EASY!
 Kathryn Murray

How often do you watch interactions between individuals and ask yourself, "Why is that person so controlling? What are they afraid of? Why do they have to be so dismissive, abusive, and aggressive?" Why do you think the victims of these behaviors put up with the abuse?

Well, I believe we see the answers some of those questions in the previous chapters. We can especially understand why some individuals feel controlling, demeaning, and abusive behavior is all they deserve. I once watched a video on Facebook; it captured an adult male absolutely beating a young, maybe five or six-year-old boy, within an inch of his life. It was horrifying, and I couldn't watch the whole thing.

The images stayed with me, and I was sickened in my spirit.

What was remarkable was that each time this father/predator/abuser hurt the child; the little boy would lift his hands up to the monster to be held. But it did not matter, that father would wind up again to some further level of violence. There was a younger child sitting next to the victim, and a baby in diapers on the couch, and someone was videotaping this atrocity (Who? The mother?) I just couldn't stand it!

Why would anyone want at record of such evil? It was just heart wrenching and despicable. But we humans have such evil within us. Maya Angelou said that all human activity is possible in all humans, and I believe her. What will that child be capable of if he survives into adulthood? He has experienced a monster creating another monster. It happens all the time, and that cycle is something that must be broken, in order to raise a generation free from such horrible training and education.

Perhaps you have heard the statistics about domestic abuse, but if not, know that it takes an abuse victim an average of seven tries before finally mustering the courage to leave the abusive situation. All the while their friends and family are wondering why they put up with the assaults, insults, and dangerous controlling behavior. I have watched enough Dr. Phil episodes where the controller (usually male but not always) reveals his snarky self in front of millions of television viewers.

I marvel at these episodes.

Do they hear their words and recognize how stupid and crazy they sound? The answer is no. The inner dialog is so real to them that they have no critical distance between their thoughts and their words. It is Dr. Phil's job to sort that out in his own distinctive Texan and highly-rated way. "So, how's that working for ya?" one of my favorite quotes.

But the abuser usually talks about how the victim is his and he has a right to treat her anyway he wants. And if she wasn't so stupid, fat, ugly, slow, foolish etc. he wouldn't have to be in her face all the time. He wouldn't have to hit her, restrict her, and direct her all the time. It is really all her fault that he has to be so controlling. She's a stupid bitch and nobody else would ever want her; it is his burden to bear…really? Really! I marvel at the BIG REVEAL this individual is giving on national television. As the camera pans the audience you see own open jaw and incredulity mirrored in faces of the studio audience.

It is easy to feel a little superior to the people on the show, but the truth is there is a lot of truth revealed in programs like Dr. Phil. The reason he is popular is because people recognize that they themselves are more than a little screwed up. Hopefully, they can get some answers there. They see themselves and others in the topics on the show; it is human drama, and anything one human does is capable of being done by other humans.

This type of programming is a safe place to view topics without doing any of the work involved. All of that is part of the instant nature of the culture at present; if we want it; we want it now.

We even want our emotional and spiritual issues fast tracked and neatly packaged; easy to access and easy digest. Now anyone who has ever done any serious rehabilitation and restoration work knows that it just isn't so. Personal growth is jagged and slow and there is much fear to be overcome in the process of excavating an authentic self.

AND IT ISN'T EASY!

But what I see in programs like Dr. Phil. is SHAME-BASED individuals, afraid of intimacy, and the BIG REVEAL of their own belief that they are flawed and unlovable at the core. They are trying desperately to control their own fear of exposure, by controlling everything they can in their own lives.

This is a pattern of human behavior called SHAME-FEAR-CONTROL. It is a very core response in human interactions.

I am reminded of the story of the Garden of Eden. Adam and Eve had done something wrong and they feared discovery of their nakedness – which they became aware of because of their actions. They attempted to cover themselves before their disobedience and SHAME was revealed by creating clothing with leaves.

We are still walking out the primordial pattern in our lives, especially in our most intimate and potentially revealing relationships.

Chaos Eaters

It is interesting to me that in a lot of the scenarios presented on programs like Dr. Phil the abuser seemed a good person during the dating and pre-commitment phase of the relationship, but after marriage or moving in together, that all changed. Many times, we find out he became a Dr. Jekyll to his Mr. Hyde. That is not surprising really because in a marriage there are very few places to hide; everything is revealed. If you are desperately afraid of the reveal the intimacy will bring you will fight being found naked and broken (the basis of fear of SHAME) and attempt to control the effect of intimacy, be setting up rules and regulations and parameters that you can control.

This usually means those closest to you, your spouse, and children, will be subject to your demands. Is this a bitter cycle. SHAME makes you feel constantly that you are worthless and unlovable; intimacy threatens to reveal that to those you want to have in your life so you begin to CONTROL the way they can interact with you in order that you are not exposed, that is a pretty scary and desperate state of affairs.

Additionally, if a person comes into a relationship from an abusive home or life experiences, they feel that abuse is all they are worthy of. The abusive situation will feel familiar to them no matter what their friends say and no matter terribly they suffer.

Sometimes this sort of abusive behavior has, through early life experiences, been perverted into what they believe is love. It isn't love of course, but Shame-based people constantly self-sabotage.

They will be comfortable in the most abusive situations because they really believe that is all they deserve. They would find it strange to believe that they had the right to demand better treatment and fairness in their relationships. That is why they remain in toxic relationships which is a mystery to their friends and loved ones. That type of Chaos is default in their lives.

QUESTIONS

Why do you think people stay in abusive or destructive relationships so long?

Why do you think people fall into SHAME-FEAR-CONTROL pattern?

What drives the cycle of shame and control? How can you recognize it?

CHAPTER SEVEN: OFFENSE – THE GO TO JAIL FREE CARD

Forgiveness is a huge risk for many people, especially if they have so much of their personal story invested in the tale of their offense and wounding. The prospect of shedding the robe of offense is a fearful prospect for many because it covers so many lost opportunities and missed moments of grace. Many feel forgiving is the same as forgetting. If they forgive, they feel that they would be accepting or even condoning the behavior of those who hurt them. Their current state of unforgiveness immortalizes the injury they have received and define them and their struggles. People, in fact, love their stories. They love to tell their stories because they feel it helps explain their behaviors and give them a unique identity. But what they fail to realize is that unforgiveness holds them in a state of suspended agitation.
Kathryn Ann Murray

I am always surprised at how casually we treat the subject of offense; it isn't really given the gravitas it deserves and yet the effects of offense and the long range even generational repercussions are so crippling.

Have you ever spoke to a bitter person and really listened to their story?

At the root cause of that bitterness in their spirit and lives will invariably be traced back to an offense taken and internalized in their lives.

The shape shifting nature of offense is such that an individual can be left with the devastating effects of bitterness and hardness in their lives and not even be aware where the root cause entered in. The lens of bitterness tends to become all-encompassing and permanent.

How many relationships have been ruined because of an offense taken that was never reconciled? Some families carry the effects of offense for generations; think of the Hatfields and the Mccoys.

Think of the root causes for many wars but getting a little closer to home think of the things that cause divisions among your family and friends. There is something very human in our ability to be offended and even more human not to seek a resolution to an offense.

Offense will embolden us to carry grudges, hatred, and malice and ill –will as if it were a badge of honor; it is slippery that way. We can accuse and excuse ourselves out of all manner of bad behaviors because "so and so" did "such and such "to me and we remember it.

No, not just remember; we encapsulate it and pass it along to whoever will listen and create an inflexible, intolerant, fixed place for that individual or individuals; frozen in time and memorial without the benefit of discussion or hope of reconciliation.

Chaos Eaters

Offense is a big devil and we give it too much power over our lives and our relationships; the active presence and authority of offense in our lives creates CHAOS. Unchecked offense will multiple, fester and take root in our lives and in the lives of every person that we have contact with. Offense and Bitterness go hand in hand and if we fail to recognize the power offense in our lives, we make ourselves subject to emotional and spiritual captivity.

The best book I have ever read on the subject of offense is John Bevere's "Bait of Satan."

In that book there is a concept which explains so clearly the nature of offense in hunting terms. The 0ffense (scanalon in Greek) refers to the spike in a trap the hunters will use to capture their prey. It is the meat put on the spike to allure the animal to come into the jaws of the trap and be captured.

Offense is that meat, the bait if you will. When the animal takes the bait, it is captured; it is simple as that. Now if the trap happened to break off the chain that held it in place the animal would still be caught no matter how far it would be able to move from the original place where it took the bait…the trap moves with that animal no matter how free it may think it is. It is caught and is dragging the trap with them wherever it happens to go until it is loosed from the trap or it dies.

That is how offense works in our lives when we allow ourselves to be offended, we are caught in the trap.

Now we do to like to see ourselves that way; we have a sense of righteousness that wants the person who offended us to be punished and take the effects of the offense. The irony is that the offender is free and the offended is captive.

Someone said that taking offense and retaining offense is like drinking poison and expecting the other person to die and it is! We see that as inherently unfair, which it is, and will keep drinking the poisonous effects of the offense getting increasing bitter because the offender is not dropping over dead or even recognizing the enormity of the offense, they perpetrated on us.

We will also share that poison with others in our attempts to rationalize our captivity. We want others to agree with us that the offender is wrong and that we are right and so we enmesh them in our captivity offering them the same bait that captured us. Misery does love company and so when offense and bitterness is allowed to operate unchecked in our lives it will ensnare others.
That is how offense and bitterness work. Yes! It is unfair. And, yes, it does not seem right that people can offend you and go free leaving you holding the bag emotionally, but remember; it is you holding the bag.

I have encountered people holding those sad, little emotional bags with countless offenses that cause them to peddle their sad stories as a way to rationalize why they are the way they are and act the way they do. They are perennial victims of the influences and offense received of others.

Chaos Eaters

You have meet them too and they wear you out with their story, especially if they have no intention of ever giving it up and being free of the consequences. Perhaps as you are reading this you see that you are carrying your own little bags of offense and bitterness.

When you see really see the devastating effects of holding offense, grudges, and bitterness in your life; that is a good day. It is finally an opportunity to free yourself from the emotional and spiritual captivity you have sentenced yourself to. But the question is, "Okay I realize that I am in an emotional and spiritual prison because of offense, but how do I get out? "Most of us do not like the answer because it flies against our notion of what is fair but it is straight forward and clear; the answer is Forgiveness!

I can hear the collective groan as I write this. "Forgiveness! Why do I have to forgive? I am not the one who is wrong, they, he, she, it should be asking forgiveness of me!" Yah! Probably! But remember you are the one that is prison and forgiveness is the only key out of there, so watcha' gonna do?

Are you going to keep protesting your unfair condition through the bars of your cell or are you going to accept the only key to your freedom? It's your choice; it was your choice to pick up the offense and it is your choice to lay it down.

Forgiveness a huge risk for many people, especially if they have so much of their personal story invested in their tale of offense.

The prospect of shedding the robe of offense is a fearful process for many because it has covered so many lost opportunities and missed moments of grace., Many fears the nakedness they many would feel without the false covering that offense seems to provide to them. Many feel that forgiving is the same as forgetting.

If they forgive, they will be accepting or even condoning the behaviors of those who hurt them and brought them to their present state. Their continued state of unforgiveness immortalizes the injury they have received and define them and their struggle.

People in fact, love their stories! They love to tell their stories because they feel it helps explain their behaviors and give them a unique identity. But what they fail to realize is that unforgiveness holds them in a suspended state of agitation.

There is a story in the bible which I often use to illustrate this point. The pool was believed to be troubled by angels at certain seasons and the first person into the pool at these times was cured. The man in this story could not move fast enough to be the first one into the pool and as the story goes, he did not have anyone to help him when the water was stirred. He had sat in this condition for over thirty-eight years! But one day Jesus came by and asked the man a simple question…" Would you be healed?" The man did not hear the question, or recognize the opportunity.

Instead, he began to tell Jesus his sad story.

Chaos Eaters

You see, his story defined him. He was that guy at the pool for thirty-eight years, who was infirm, invalid, and friendless. I would venture to say, that everyone that came to that pool in hope of a cure knew this guy's story and were more than a little tired of it; truth be told.

So instead of answering the question that Jesus had asked him the man did what he always did; he began to tell his sad story. Fortunately for him, Jesus got past his story and gave him his miracle almost against his will..." Arise, take up your bed and get out of this condition! Really, he was saying, "Give up your sad story and get delivered from your past; quit letting your sad story define you."

How many people do you know like this guy? His story is not uncommon. People want to tell you why they are the way they are.

Why they are stuck, and why they are not responsible? But they fail to recognize that their story is a jail cell. I have seen people try to put a brave face or even a false humility over their tales of woe and even paste scriptures over the situation. But all of that activity is just decorating a jail cell; no matter how you try to cover the walls of your prison you are still bound; you are still a prisoner

What is necessary in these situations is the key to the cell door and that key, the only key, is forgiveness. I understand how difficult that is for some of you to receive. Many of you have suffered unspeakable and horrendous woundings in your life and you think that your anger and outrage is the only think that has brought you through.

But there are terrible consequences to that internalized turmoil in your life; emotionally, physically, and spiritually.

I want to present an alternative which leads to peace and reconciliation.

The way is forgiveness, period; if you have tried everything else and are still none better, what do you have to lose here? Accept a prison sentence and bitterness and the resultant chaos that disrupts and manipulates your life.

When I relate these things, believe me, I have not been immune from the effects of offense and bitterness in my life. It is the human experience and it is my personal experience as well. I had to do forgiveness work for my family especially, my father as the result of his alcoholism and suicide.

I have had to forgive members of my family as they have had to forgive me. When we cannot forgive, we are stuck, it is as simple as that. When we internalize offense, we remain frozen in time in that relationship and carry the burden of the offense into every part of our lives. What I know is the best thing I can do for MYSELF is to be quick to forgive any offending parties in my life. It is a discipline worth learning as it produces peace, health, and liberty in my life.

And guess what? Life gives you a lot of opportunities to practice forgiveness because offense is a continuing part of the landscape of all of our lives. At one time, I realized that I had gotten pretty good at practicing offense and bitterness with disastrous results.

Still, I have also apprehended that learning to forgive, and receiving the benefits from forgiveness, have been great liberators in my life. The discipline of forgiveness, and walking in the grace of it has given me a peace and compassion that I never had before. This awareness and discipline have not come without a price, but offense and bitterness exact a terrible price as well, without remedy. We get to choose the pharaohs in our lives.

In the formational days of the ministry, I am still a part of, there were about twelve women that were gathered together in those organizational days. Those twelve women were about as disparate as a group can be; different temperaments, different levels of wounding, different levels of maturity and they all came with a different vision of the task at hand.

We decided to try a different sort of organizational structure, less hierarchal, more relational, and circular; we called it a "table top" organizational style. Rather than have a single vision and a single leader in a kind of top down structure; we attempted to give everyone at the table a voice and a vote. We tried to do everything by consensus which meant that the task was less important than the relationships that were being developed in the process. Believe me, for some of the Cholerics in the group (including me), the discipline of that organizational structure was difficult.

But what happened over time was that the whole group took ownership of any activity we had consensus on and each was able to contribute to the success of the undertaking according to their own giftings and talents.

In the process, around that table, we mutually discovered the giftings and talents of the women gathered there. As a group, we were able to activate and encourage every member of the group to first have a voice and accept the responsibility of the group's mission. But still there was conflict and offense even when our motto was "Relationships are the most important thing!"

Yup! Relationships are the most important thing but they are messy and a consensus model of management is unwieldy.

The pro-relational sentiment served us well as a group and we learned a lot about each other, the nature of relationships and leadership but not without offense. The opportunity for offense was always present, as a result we created another motto for the group, we pledged, "Not to take or give offense BUT when offense came, we pledged to be quick to forgive."

Believe me, we were exercised by that pledge over the years and not without failing, often glaringly and sometimes irreparably.

In my discussions of the personality types you will remember that the Melancholy temperament is blessed with an incredible memory including an ability to keep a running tab of faults and offenses. Choleric types are not really all that concerned with feelings and are not really very approachable as they consider criticism as disloyalty. So, when a Melancholy personality has to deal a Choleric for any length of time there is an opportunity for a fairly long list of offenses.

Chaos Eaters

If the long-suffering Melancholy does not choose to discuss the offenses as they come up, the list will create a breaking point and an eruption of feeling from which it is really hard to recover.

In chapter three, I discussed the Personality Stepping Stone, or Stumbling Block. Remember the Green Stamp Redemption Center?

Despite our best efforts to make" relationships the most important thing" and" not to give or take offense" members of the group had serious conflicts and breaking points. I had a very influential and incredibly contributing member of that original group present a multipage, single- spaced litany of my offenses and faults to me in my own living room; it was not pretty and that incident underscored our relationship for years afterward.

You just do not pull immediately up from that sort of experience and without forgiveness those life experiences our irreparable. My friend and I have since reconciled. We love each other and appreciate the incredible roles we played in each other's lives at that pivotal and important season, but our relationship has never been the same since that afternoon in my living room. I had another co-laborer, friend and long-term ministry partner who chose to divest herself of her involvement in the ministry and by consequence, me, over the phone on a beautiful October afternoon.

I can still remember where I was that day and where I pulled off the road to take it all in, after she hung up on me when I tried to get to the bottom of her feelings.

That development came incidentally, after the ministry had enjoyed one of its most important and effective opportunities at a state-wide women's conference.

In fact, when she called that afternoon, I really thought she wanted to discuss how well the meeting had gone and how effective the team had been. Her husbands' health had kept her home from the venue. Imagine how blind-sided I was at that moment; it took my breath away especially since I considered her my best friend at the time. Those situations are always hard to endure without struggling with offense/bitterness but it is in those crucibles that you sharpen your resolve to forgive because you must to go on and be free.

I share these personal stories because we all have similar opportunities in our lives and the discipline of forgiveness is the only key out of a potential incarceration; the jail cell of rejection, offense and bitterness is always open. I would love to report that those relationships I talked about here have returned to the robust state they once were but that is not the case. I am glad to say the both those relationships, once so dear and integral in my life have morphed into a more nuanced and distant respect and appreciation for all the things and opportunities that we shared. We have all moved forward in our individual destinies.

I would like to think each of us would say we would not be where we are today without the influences and relationships, we shared in those important life seasons, but we were all tested in the fire. You will too. But always remember in those times, if forgiveness is not active in your life, offense will always be your go to jail free card.

QUESTIONS

What are some ways you are carrying your own little bags of offense and bitterness?

Where have you become stuck because your sad story defines you?

Who are the two (or three) people you most need to forgive?

CHAPTER EIGHT: OFFENSE WILL COME...

NOT MY CIRCUS NOT MY MONKIES - Polish Proverb

I addressed the issue of offense earlier in this book and also mentioned a great book on the subject called "The Bait of Satan "by John Bevere. But the point I am trying to make by adding to the discussion of the subject of offense is its resoluteness ...offense is inevitable!

IT WILL COME AND WE ARE ALL SUSCEPTIBLE TO THE POWERFUL NEGATIVE INFLUENCE IT TRIES TO EXERT IN OUR LIVES.

It is important to address this point because the final result of unresolved offense is BITTERNESS. Bitterness is a dandelion-rooted kind of force. If you don't get rid of the problem of offense at the roots; the seeds of that offense will spread all over the acreage of your life and sadly the lives of everyone you are in contact with.

I live in a fairly manicured and well-maintained development at the present time. The association that I pay dues to, makes sure that our yards are fertilized, sprayed for weeds, and mowed. I love that arrangement, because for a small fee I have a nicely maintained yard without any personal involvement at all.

Unfortunately, there is an empty lot that adjoins our development that is a breeding ground for all sorts of noxious weeds, and the owner (a bank with no real attachment to the property) is very careless about the whole sorry mess.

So, by the time our association has complained enough to prompt a mowing by the bank; the weeds have been allowed to complete their entire life cycle and have seeded themselves everywhere including our adjoining well maintained property. It is really annoying to all of us, but there is little we can do.

We maintain our own noxious weed problem but others less vigilant still affect our quality of life in our little cul-de-sac world. I use that as an illustration because there are people in your life that do not maintain their noxious weed life and are constantly trying to seed their negativity into your life.

You can probably think of a few such individuals right now. Unfortunately, many of the individuals can be as close as family, work relationships and even friends. So, what can we do with these influences?

Often escaping their negative influence is as improbable as moving our housing development from noxious weed factory next to our properties. The seeds will come; that is inevitable but allowing the seeds to root in our lives is our choice.

Just like we are forced to be vigilant with the spread of noxious seeds in our yards we have to be vigilant about the people in our lives who want to spread negativity and seeds of bitterness in our lives.

We not only have to be aware of our offenses taken but the effects of the active offenses in other people's lives which want to spread their seeds of bitterness and negativity into our manicured lives because it produces chaos.

Be vigilant because listening to every bitter heart will affect your world and it often will mask itself as a compassionate Christian thing to do...dare I say a "calling." If you are not careful, your peace will be robbed in a false sense of Christian duty.

I have met individuals that truly are "the black hole" of emotional need; there really is no end to the depths of the needs that they want you to carry for them and feel a false sense of responsibility for them. And if you do not present a solution to their issues that only they can really resolve themselves, often those individuals will get upset with you and accuse you of being unsympathetic and un-Christian. That is a core issue in the co-dependency cycle someone wants to make you feel responsible for their issues and you pick up that responsibility with really no way to affect permanent remedy.

There is also a very tricky version of Offense which I have come to label, "The Double Whammy." What is that? Let me explain, there is something in human communication which is called triangulation, which very simply introduces a third person into a discussion that really should be handled between the two people who are having issues. Why do people do that? Mainly because it is easier to talk about an issue with an uninvolved third person than it is to confront the issue with the person directly involved. Most often we are careful to select a sympathetic ear to air our grievances.

We want them to agree with our point of view and be on our side in a conflict which is frankly none of their business.

But we make it their business and often make agreement of our assessment of the situation a condition of our continued friendship and intimacy.

So, the person we are enveloping in our conflict is beginning to be enveloped in the first loop of the Double Whammy, agree with me, or lose our friendship. It really is a form of emotional blackmail and puts a lot of pressure on the third party to agree and often there is an expectation to agree with our point of view heartily and enthusiastically. Let's face it you must be emotionally mature to withstand such a full court press, especially if that relationship is a mainstay in your life.

Be careful, because if you buy into the conflict by a tacit and enthusiastic agreement it is like the old story of Brier Rabbit. In that story there is a tar baby…a baby covered in tar, don't ask; it is a fable and it works for illustration here.

The point is, if you try to rescue that Tar Baby your hand will get stuck if tar and if you try to free yourself from the tar you will have both hands and both feet attached to the Tar Baby in the struggle; stuck, but good. Borrowing Offense from someone else is like trying to rescue that Tar Baby, you, will get stuck in the process. I have a favorite expression of late, it says, "Not my circus, not my monkeys!"

To rephrase that in context of the fable and the subject at hand "Not my tar, not my baby!" Buy into the conflict and the tar baby/offense becomes your conflict and offense. In addition, the two individuals having the conflict will often resolve their issues, and leave you holding the proverbial "bag."

Chaos Eaters

You were not involved in the matter first hand, but now you are left with opinions, feelings and chemistry affecting your life, attitude, and peace of mind. It is a Double Whammy, for sure!

It is hard enough to keep yourself offense free, and discipline yourself with the necessary forgiveness to make that happen, but when you take on offense for others you pollute your own peace of mind with no real way of addressing the underlying issues. You have borrowed trouble and dis-ease and chaos. We may believe we are being a loyal friend; but we are really touching a Tar Baby and will suffer for it. I have seen this at work in my life, and have lost friendships because I did not understand the entrapment of borrowing offense, or the impact my life.

These experiences are very painful, and deadly serious so it it's important to always ask yourself when called to pick up an offense in the name of friendship…

Is it *your* Circus? Are they really *your* monkeys?

The best course of action is to listen without commitment. Encourage reconciliation and resolution between those with skin in the game. It helps me from tending noxious weeds in my soul and spirit that were not my planting or my responsibility to manage.

QUESTIONS

Where have unaddressed or unresolved offenses become BITTERNESS?

Who are the "noxious weed" people you have allowed to grow? How are they affecting your quality of life?

Name potential ways you can escape from their negative influence in your life.

CHAPTER NINE: ESTABLISHING A LANGUAGE OF RECOVERY

"The business of language formation is serious business. Consider that someone who cannot speak is called "dumb." Finding a voice to express and communicate our needs, opinions and observations is the basic formational process of our young years. Isn't it true that we admire someone who can really express themselves well? There is a power in it."
Kathryn Murray

I love the statement, "words are the voice of the heart". A paperweight with that inscription has been on my desk for years. The significance of that statement has become more and more precious to me as I have fought to process my feelings and develop a language of recovery. A friend of mine has described that process as "root-cause analysis" I do not think that expression is original to her but it was new to me. It allowed me to have an umbrella under which I could place a lot of my thoughts and ideas. Language sets apart from all other life forms.

Now I realize that all of creation communicates but only humans write down their ideas and dialog about intentions, feelings, hopes, accomplishments, failures and the elusive concept of personal growth and destiny.

We do not come out of the womb with the ability to communicate our inner most thoughts and aspirations; but we are born with the potential to gain the language to do so.

We start with cries and cooing and baby talk and develop language over time and with experience. The trouble with the process is that it takes time and it is full of trial and error.

We all laugh at the crazy things that come out of children's mouths as they develop their language skills. For the most part, all of it is adorable accept when they repeat the word, they have heard which is totally inappropriate and embarrassing to the parents.

Children do not know what is appropriate; they do not police their language. They are just busy learning how to describe and communicate with their world. Their language development will reflect the environment in which it develops. Children have not yet learned the subtlety of the processes. They have to learn to prevaricate, deflect, camouflage, and hide in their language. They have to learn that some words are inappropriate and bad. And children do not have the language and ability to describe quality of their life experience positive or negative.

Whatever they experience in those early years becomes their emotional bedrock; whatever is written on their souls, which I call the mind, will and emotions in those years becomes the root for their behaviors in the future.

If they are given a safe, supportive, and loving environment to explore their early investigations and experience they will be more likely to have a positive and confident view of their place in the world. And the converse is also true; if children grow up in a negative, abusive, neglectful, and hurtful home, they will tend to have a negative, fearful, and angry view of themselves and their place in the world. This not rocket science, just rudimentary psychology. I do not present this concept as a breakthrough, but for some this will be a breakthrough.

Adults often try to live a life as if their childhood never happened and cannot understand why their lives do not work. They are puzzled why they recreate the dysfunctional patterns of their childhood when they were so determined that they would never become their parents. They are amazed and discouraged that they see themselves reflecting the behaviors they swore they would never model to their children.

Some experts would call these passed on behavior systems, "the sins of the fathers". I would agree with that, but whether you believe in the concept of sin or not, you have to realize that some thoughts, patterns, behaviors, and beliefs are toxic and cause an individual distress and brokenness. Why do we allow these behaviors to color our lives and relationships?

I think there are several factors involved. It is very difficult to admit that a pattern of behavior or thinking is wrong; it makes us feel "less than". We often just excuse those parts of our person by just saying, "That is just the way I am! Deal with it!"

Have you ever heard yourself or someone else say, "Well I am German, Italian, Irish, Russian, or whatever."? There is type of behavior and expectations associated with each of those nationalities, isn't there? And often our more negative behaviors are presented as the status quo; that is just the way it is.

It is much easier to explain away our mistakes, behaviors, and attitudes than to confront them and begin the process of self-examination and change. There is real fear in that and that fear of exposure keeps us bound. Shakespeare said this in his play Hamlet when his main character says, while pondering the meaning of life, "...Better bear those ills we have, then run to those we know not of".

The business of language formation is serious business; consider that someone who cannot speak is called dumb. Finding a voice to express and communicate our needs, opinions, and our observations is the basic formational process of our young years. What children hear becomes the building blocks of their world. We define our world and our experiences by words. Words bring us into the circle of human interaction. Isn't true that we admire someone who can really express themselves well?

There is a power in it. There is even a belief that if you can define a situation with words you can control it. Something you can talk about and define loses much of its power. Think about those times when you really feel that you have successfully got your point across to someone else, when there is that look of understanding and reception from another human being. It is satisfying isn't?

Chaos Eaters

It is important that we understand that right alongside the business of language formation there is another very powerful platform being built in our lives. That platform is our experiences and the feelings attached to those experiences. I often say that feelings are real but they are not necessarily true.

Those first experiences in our early development are some of the most potent influences in our lives. Everything that happens in those formative years are the first strokes on the canvas of our lives. They count; it is sort of the emotional DNA that we will use to define all our experiences going forward. Child psychologists tell us that the first three years of lives are absolutely critical to the formation of a child's ongoing sense of well-being and ability to thrive. That really gives me pause especially in light of all the terrible things that we hear that happens to children these days.

No home is perfect, there will always be issues, but some homes are absolutely toxic. What the child of those environments experience will leave them with feelings that will define them the rest of their days. That is the worst-case scenario. I really believe that all of us pick up unexamined and potentially debilitating feelings in our formative years; it is part of the process.

The problem is that feelings that are not examined become the bedrock of who we believe we are. Feelings are real buggers; they present themselves as the true even when they are crippling and debilitating. The problem with those early feelings is that they have been with us so long that they feel like they belong; they are allowed to define us.

Not only do we feel powerless over them, we accept those feelings as the status quo. We see them as who we really are without examining the roots of their genesis in our lives.

Just as we develop a vocabulary to describe the physical world around us, I propose that we need to develop a vocabulary for the inner workings of our soul; especially in those areas we are bound by the tyranny of negative feelings about ourselves. Wow! That is a scary proposal, isn't?

The truth of the matter is that most of us are, to varying degrees mute/dumb in the areas of our emotional underpinnings, especially where long term negative feelings are concerned. Why would we want to evaluate things that would expose ourselves in a negative light? We keep those things close to our chests and out of sight of the casual observer.

Often, we keep those things covered even in our closest and most intimate relationships. But the problem is that it takes a lot of effort to keep those things under control. Those feelings seem to have a life of their own and show out in embarrassing and unpredictable ways. And the longer we are in a relationship which demands transparency and honesty, the more uncomfortable we can become.

The truth is that we usually are not prompted to explore those feelings unless there is a crisis of some kind; depression, the loss of a loved one, a broken relationship, suicidal thoughts, and the like.

But sometimes we are just sick and tired of the work to maintain the façade and the struggle to subdue feelings which just seem to rule us. We do not have a language to deal with these feelings because we have thought, wrongfully, that they are us at the core. It is as simple as that and we are afraid that what we fear is true.

However, when things simply do not work and we see a repetitive pattern of self-sabotage, we are forced to explore the inner landscape of our souls and search out the root causes for our behavior. It is scary work and necessary. We desperately need a vocabulary of recovery to help us tame and control the seemingly uncontrollable feelings and impulses in our life. Just as we needed a vocabulary to define and communicate the physical world when we were children.

Today if someone would describe themselves as an adult child of an alcoholic, I would understand immediately what they were communicating. But that wasn't always the case, I had to explore my life and my feelings in light of the fact that I had been raised in the home of an alcoholic. Every child thinks that their home is normal even if it's dysfunctional.

What do they have to measure it by? They only have their own experience. So, my process of recovery had to deal with my father's alcoholism and how his behaviors left residual feelings in my soul. Feelings which had to be identified and labeled so that I could separate what was his life from what were my feelings about myself because of his addiction. I did not know that the feeling I had of somehow being responsible for his addiction was called co-dependence.

I did not know the alcoholism affects the whole family. I didn't know that my mother's excuses and cover-ups for my father's behavior was called enablement.

I not realize that I patterned her behavior in my relationships with men. I did not know that the deep feeling of worthlessness and brokenness, of feeling that I was a mistake was called Shame. All these feelings were at work in my life holding me back, defining me making me feel inadequate.

No matter what success I had I lived in fear of exposure that someone would see through my façade and see that I was somehow wrong at my core. I was afraid of that rejection but I did not understand how deeply the fear ruled my life. It was exhausting to constantly be presenting a positive image I felt was a sham that could be exposed at any minute. But when I began to explore my feelings in the context of my home experience, I began to get free. I began to acquire a vocabulary of recovery. That language formation was every bit as essential as my words to communicate the dimensions of my observations in the physical world.

There is another aspect of the dysfunctional home has to be addressed because it encourages silence and secrets instead of communication. The nature of a dysfunctional home is the dynamic of the lie which must be believed. Everyone involved is a sworn directly or indirectly to the pact of secrecy. Many of you will recognize this in the phrase that is so often used in these situations, 'What happens at home, stays at home!"

There is a code of silence in these situations.

Often a perpetrator will silence a victim with a threat to harm them or the other people in their lives. But even if child recognizes that something is not quite right in their circumstances, their concerns are often dismissed adding to the confusion in their minds. Something else happens too, if the big people in your life are telling that something is a certain way, you believe them even if it goes against what you feel. That causes a doubt and a dismissal of your own view of reality which makes you begin to distrust your own fledging view of the world. I have a friend who is just beginning to recover her own voice.

She was a victim of incest and sexual abuse when she was very young.

Now years later she can see that those early childhood experiences caused her to doubt not only her own worth but also the value of her thoughts and words. She will admit today that the feelings of helplessness and powerlessness in those early years took her voice away from her. She hid for years behind a kind of chalkboard which allowed anyone to write things on her which she seemed powerless to do anything about. She really was emotionally mute. She would think things in her mind that she felt powerless to convey, and hid herself and did what was expected of her for years.

As she began her own root-cause analysis she could see the where that feeling of powerlessness entered in and she could walk through her life and her experiences with a critical and understanding vocabulary. She began the process of releasing her voice by using the words of recovery.

She is amazed that her thoughts and words have authority and power. She is amazed that her feelings are validated and although having an authentic voice is still new to her; she is reveling in her new liberty. My friend's story illustrates what I call the language of recovery. She was able to sort out the feelings of her early life experiences and acquire words that tamed the feelings that ruled her life.

It is an encouragement to each of us that feel mute and frustrated by feelings that seem to rule over us without hope of deliverance. We can gain power over those feelings. We can use the language of recovery to build a new platform for our lives. And in turn we can express the journey to others who are still caught mute and unable to separate those negative debilitating feelings from their own definition of who they are and what they are capable of, because words really are the language of the heart.

QUESTIONS

Where is it difficult to admit that a pattern of behavior or thinking is wrong in your life?

How have unexamined feelings become the bedrock of who you believe you are?

Strategize ways you can separate negative feelings from your definition of who you are?

CHAPTER TEN: MY STORY... EVERYONE HAS ONE!

"Slowly, I began to acquire a vocabulary for my journey and those words had power; they still do. That is the genesis of this book and sharing my own journey is my way of being honest with my readers. Nothing I am presenting in this book is just good material. It is really a document of my personal emotional and spiritual recovery."
Kathryn Murray

The depression that had plagued me for so many years had a very deep hold on me and this was AFTER my conversion experience with Christ. That was really what was so confusing; I had felt such a release and new beginning in my new relationship with Christ but still secret feelings of brokenness and unworthiness even in the face of the great grace permeated my life. I feared many things at that time; the greatest fear was that my new found life in Christ was an illusion and if it was... I had no hope.

My generation had chased a" new reality" for years on the road, in drugs, relationships, shedding old systems and embracing new ones. It was a serial pursuit running on and on to the next" new thing" without restraint and then disillusioned seeking yet another "new thing." So, my fractured heart was at war with my new life in Christ and I feared that the fractures and hidden brokenness was going to win.

My father had been an alcoholic all of his life, and the darkness of his demons and depression finally claimed his life, when he died a suicide on June 4th, 1971.

That event was always close to my emotional life; I feared that I would end up with the same sense of hopelessness. I remembered standing in the funeral home next to my father's body. I was holding his hand and cursing a lot but then I made a curious promise to him, I promised that I would find "it "for both of us.

Truth was I was clueless about what "it" was: and that statement was more a stab at the darkness of the whole experience than any confidence that I had in my abilities to discover a reality to sustain my life and explain his desperation. In fact, my new experience in Christ began after a very serious bout with depression that almost took my life at 27.

Now forty years later as a believer and disciple of Christ, I can see the hand of God over decades of His faithfulness. In the chapter on Shame I told you the story of my Shame awakening. It was at my sister's house in Sioux City. That was the beginning of a new day of understanding for me. I did not realize that at the time, driving home that evening the future looked as dark as the South Dakota sky ahead me. But a new day was dawning.

It started the very next morning with a call from an acquaintance of mine. I did not even know this woman very well and the conversation didn't last long. She told me that she felt "led" to give me a referral. The referral was the name of a local counselor in Sioux Falls.

Chaos Eaters

I had had a successful experience with counseling before and so I was willing to give this woman a try. I made the appointment and began the journey out of SHAME and the staggering effects of a dysfunctional early childhood experiences. I could not have known then that my issues were common to children raised in an alcoholic or dysfunctional home.

The power of SHAME is isolation and fear of exposure; that lie which reinforces the silence and the belief that "you are the only one that feels this way, everyone else is okay." That is of course exactly what I was feeling that evening at my sister's home. There is a real push me-pull me in that sort of shame-based breakdown, you desperately need someone to get past your emotional shut down, and stuckness, but at the same time you are petrified that when they do, they will see the real heart of the situation and reject you.

The process of recovering my childhood self was very challenging. It involved facing boarded up rooms that I had avoided for years. I was afraid of opening those places; they always led to bouts of depression and self-loathing. In this fullness of time however, NOT examining those hurt and broken places was more painful then avoiding them. I found that I was ready to understand.

I found that I could walk through my fears and recover parts of myself that had been lost along the way. Slowly I began to acquire a vocabulary for my journey and those words had power and they still do. That is the genesis for this book and sharing my journey is my way of being honest with my readers.

Nothing I am presenting in this book is just good material, it has been processed in my life personally and often painfully; it really is a document of my personal emotional recovery.

For anyone who has experienced counseling you now that it really is a dialog with yourself with a friend in the room. Skilled counseling is one of the healing arts and I have received the benefits on more than one occasion. My personality veers to people pleasing -performer especially when I am uncomfortable and afraid of being rejected. I say that because I even brought that proclivity into my counseling sessions.

I remember coming into a session one afternoon just really angry. I didn't feel I had anything interesting or funny or worthwhile to talk about and I felt exposed. If I had nothing to contribute, what good was I? I came in a temper and told the counselor that I didn't feel particularly bright or clever that day and that she had to just get used to it

BECAUSE I WAS PAYING HER and she had to do her job even if I didn't have anything particularly interesting or clever to bring to the session.

I was stunned when the counselor complimented me on getting in touch with my anger and then proceeded to tell me that I did not have to worry about being loved or received in the sessions because she had already decided to love me!

What?! Without performance I was getting unconditional love; that isn't how it worked in my world.

In my whole life I had been rewarded for being extroverted, bright and entertaining; it was one of the things my father had loved about me. My counselor had given me a safe place where my performance did not determine her acceptance of me. That is a lot like grace defined here as unmerited favor.

I wasn't comfortable with that concept but the more I accepted that premise in our sessions the more progress I made.

I did not realize that I had all the earmarks of an ADULT CHILD OF AN ALCOHOLIC. I did not know that there was a way of expressing all that anger and sense of failure and I wasn't aware that there were so many people in the same case with the same issues.

That was strangely comforting; I wasn't alone. All those feelings I had of failure because of my father's drinking and suicide were by product of the dysfunctional home. I came to understand that when the BIG PEOPLE fail their responsibilities, the children pick up the responsibility.

They feel that things would be better if they had been smarter, quieter, prettier and any number of "betters." Children internalize the chaos around them as a flaw in themselves. They see themselves as responsible, and get the message "things are bad in your life because you are unlovable and broken because if you weren't so flawed THE BIG PEOPLE would treat you better!"

That is the basic message of SHAME.

It is interesting what events stick to your soul as a child. For me, I remembered a Christmas shopping experience with my father. It was Christmas Eve he had come home from work; he had been drinking.

We always waited for him to get home before we opened presents. He was drinking and feeling magnanimous so he loaded us all in the car to drive to the local Lewis Drug to buy a Stereo. My Mother did not go along with us; she was upset with my Dad. In the store he was loud, which was not typical behavior for him. I could tell he thought he was very funny and generous, but I was the oldest and I hated that people were looking at us strangely.

I could see in their faces, they pitied us. I just wanted out of the place. I felt so exposed that I started to cry. My Dad just continued his intoxicated search for a new stereo, and all I wanted was to be in the car on the road back to the safety of my bedroom.

But it was the clerk who checked us out that really affected me; I could tell that my father's behavior disgusted him and he looked at us with a mixture of disdain and weak pity; I hated that.

My father was too loaded to see how he was being treated but I felt so exposed and vulnerable that I just wanted to disappear. It was like that clerk embodied all the secret fears I had about my family and me personally. His treatment of us confirmed my suspicions that there was something wrong with our family and me in particular. I can tell you that I never liked the "stereo" because it reminded me of the scalding" glass underwear" experience on Christmas Eve at Lewis Drug.

Chaos Eaters

I remembered that in counseling and realized that experience, and others like it had formed the basis for all those SHAME-based episodes in my life, amazing right? There were others that we uncovered in the counseling process.

My father was a railway engineer and back in the day there were passenger trains that connected cities in the Midwest. The Great Northern offered service between Sioux City, Iowa. and Sioux Falls, South Dakota. From there the train continued on to Willmar, St Paul, and Minneapolis, Minnesota. My family took advantage of those routes to travel to family members all over the country.

I was my daddy's favorite and so often I got to sit with him in the engine; it was a thrill for me to be up in that great machine on my daddy's lap. It was totally illegal I am sure, but it remains a great memory for me. But there was a time, that the other man in the engine, "the fireman" asked my Dad if I could sit on his lap on the other side of the engine. The engines I remember from that time were massive and there was a jutting out of the mechanics of the machine into the middle of the engine room. The engineer sat on the right side of that steel peninsula and the fireman sat on the left.

It was difficult to see the other side of the engine room, the view was obstructed and it worked to this fireman's advantage. He chose that opportunity to put his hand down my panties and fondle my private parts. All the time he was violating me, he was talking to my Dad like everything was all right, and he was showing me the sights from his side of the train.

It was horrible and confusing. I did not know what to do. By the time I got back to my father's lap all I wanted to do was join my mother and sisters in the passenger car. The whole incident made me question whether my father could take care of me. After all that entire horrible violation happened when he was in the same room with me.

Another experience should be documented here which was very subtle and confusing which involved the Parish priest, Father Brennan. You have to understand that in a Catholic household in the 1950s and 1960s, the parish priest was an individual of unique power and position. He was God's representative and authority on the earth. The priest was next to God, spoke for God, you confessed your sins to him and he made it right with God.

The parish priest was a man of singular power and influence.

My father, a non-Catholic, liked Father Brennan because he drank and smoked like a regular guy. Father Brennan had other regular guy tastes and urges; and a lot of young girls were victim to his "special attentions" Many of little girl friends had encounters with the priest that was not sacramental in nature.

My own encounter with the predator came during the Christmas Holidays in my eight-grade year. Catholic Moms at the time did not think it strange for priest to ask their young daughter to come to the rectory (the priest's residence) to help with some task or other. My Mom did not think anything of it when Father Brenan wanted me to come to the rectory and help him with a mailing. So, I was allowed to go.

Chaos Eaters

While I was there Father Brennan asked me to sit next to him at the only desk in the room uncomfortably close to him. I did, but things began to get strange because he began to remark on how beautiful my eyes where and how pretty I was. I just kept saying "Thank you, Father!"

But then he asked me if I wanted a drink and I said sure, a coke. No, he said I want to know if you want a drink; I realized that he was talking about alcohol. Now this is the same guy that talked to our class about the sin of alcohol, sex, and foul language. And now HE was offering me a drink. He got up to make drinks, and I saw my opportunity to leave.

I was so uncomfortable and intimidated. I made for the only door in the room but He caught me there and pulled me close to him brushing me against his enlarged penis. I was horrified and confused I do not remember how I got out of that place but I was so upset and unnerved. My mother noticed my state when I got home but didn't ask any questions.

Later in the Holiday season just before school would start again, Father Brennan called our home again and asked my mother if I would be available to help him with another project. My mother looked at my face and told the priest that we were in the middle of taking down Christmas decorations and that I wasn't available.

Now that may not seem remarkable, but what she said was a lie. We had already taken down Christmas decorations. My Catholic mother had lied to her priest, and I loved her for it. I really didn't look forward to returning to school and seeing Father Brennan again; in fact, I dreaded it!

The first time I saw him was at a school dance in the gymnasium/lunchroom/auditorium on the third level of the building.

I remember my first sighting of him very well. The lights had been dimmed in the auditorium for the dance but the lights were on in the hallway where some classrooms were. He came in through that light wearing a cassock (a long black garment much like a dress and his white collar). His entrance terrified me. I remember trying to shrink away from having to speak to him; I really wanted to disappear.

He however seemed to be on a mission to find me. I had pressed myself up against the mesh covering of the windows; so close to the window that I could feel the cold of the webbing beneath my clothes. Father Brennan saw me, and made his way directly to where I was standing. I had nowhere to go and felt trapped and desperate.

What he said to me there in that place was a travesty to the whole institution he represented. He asked me "If I did not know that it was a sin to lie to a priest?" Really? What a bastard! He was using every aspect of his authority as a mentor, a man, and as a priest to intimidate a little girl who had escaped his perversion.

Of course, I did not understand that then, I was shamed into silence and submission; and he was holding the "spiritual card.' He was the one who forgave my sins. What a terrible abuse of trust and position but somehow at the time I felt unclean and sinful.

It made me feel like it was MY FAULT that the parish priest had attempted to violate me, and all my spiritual constructs at the time.

Chaos Eaters

I did not go to confession with him after that, I went to Father Wingert, the homely priest. I felt more comfortable with him, and avoided Father Brennan as much as possible. There is a picture of me standing next to him at my eight-grade graduation. I am standing stiffly beside him with a smile frozen of my face and he is the picture of relaxed piety.

My father always said "He was a hell of a guy!" He was.

My ongoing relationship with my father has been the most complex relationship of my life; it continues to be. There were so many aspects of his life that impacted me; positively and negatively. Even forty-three years after his suicide, there are issues in my personal life and in the lives of our immediate family that spring directly from his influence on our lives all those many years ago.

The power of parents and adults in a young person's world is staggering; it really is! Throughout my young adult life, I felt myself drawn to men that I could fix; broken people who just needed a chance, or a savior, OR A ME to help them evolve into a perfectly whole human being. I was attracted to brilliant broken things.

I had a passion to make them better; to help them fully live. I felt I was the answer to someone's brokenness. There is a principal I discovered in this: brokenness seeks brokenness. It is what is comfortable and usual.

Brokenness seems the natural experiential way of things. It is bad training and education, but you seek out what you are familiar with. It is the root of what counselor's call co-dependence.

I learned this behavior in my home; my mother was constantly making excuses for my dad, covering up his drunken behaviors and making excuses for him. How many bouts of "flu" can one man have, right? In my relationships, I frankly put up with a lot of crap. I also loved my father and didn't realize that I was trying to rescue these other fellows I was really trying to save my Dad.

My sisters tell of a time when they were retrieving my father from a bar because he was too intoxicated to drive home. They found him a booth doubled over a drink saying" Help me, help me! "Tall order for two young girls or for a family who loved the man. The truth is we couldn't help him. We had not been equipped for such a monumental task. We had been taught to cover up, be quiet and protect the lie in the house.

In our own ways I believe that all of the women left behind in the wake of my Dad's passing all tried to save of the guys of their acquaintance. My mother's co-dependent behaviors continued almost to her death; a series of one broken man after another; it was what she was used to; her mother had taught that to her and she patterned that to us; the beat goes on as they say.

There was an additional subtle pattern of behavior that I began to see in myself. My father loved words and poetry his whole family did. He was called Shakespeare by his buddies on the railroad. He scribbled poetry on his log books and scraps of paper; we have many of those poems today and we all love them. However, as the oldest child and Dad's favorite I had felt a keen need to be my father's apologist.

Chaos Eaters

People asked my questions about him that I couldn't answer and I just sort of began to fill in the blanks. I am a thinker and a very verbal person and I have a real knack for stringing words together. I even wrote ad copy for a while. I love words and I know that comes directly from my father's influence. But for years before I would say something clever I would preface my remarks with this expression "as my father used to say..." Now my father was really a man a few words and he never did say any of those things. But I realized that I was polishing his apple, making him look better than he was.

Trying to make him wise and worthy better than his end as a suicide better than being a drunk. Those words, "a drunk" were hard for me; I preferred to label him as "alcoholic"; that seems sort of antiseptic and clinical. Alcoholism is a disease, right? Being" a drunk' denotes a moral and personal failure. I was trying to revise my father's place in the world and add to his status by giving him credit for my best thoughts, subtle, right? Still very co-dependent, revisionist behavior; an attempt to whitewash the hard reality by assigning my Dad thoughts and words he never had.

I always wanted to present him as better than his end. Telling people that your father was a suicide always prompts a strange, odd expression on people's faces. They don't usually have anything to say, unless they of course had lost a loved one in the same way; then there is a survivor's sense of knowing and a bond that embraces the unanswered questions and mystery that always remains... and the survivor guilt.

When I began to recover my own thoughts and words, I began to recover a part of my authentic self.

The process of recovery is about descending through layers and peeling back layers to expose the truth. It is difficult to remove the old coping devices and lies that have become too familiar to you. But discovering your authentic self is one of the chief joys in life. Like anything worthwhile in life, it costs a lot; old myths and lies must be defeated, the layers pulled back and discarded; work, but worth it.

I remember one session with my counselor that became the turning point in my anger issues with my father. Oh were you surprised that with all my efforts to memorialize my father, that I was angry with him? Well, don't be. I was furious with him to my core but I was always afraid to approach that rage because I really felt it would tip me over emotionally.

My Counselor had told me the week before that it was time for "a LONG SESSION." I did not like the sound of that, it sounded ominous and scary and out of the ordinary weekly sessions. I reluctantly agreed. Although I really wasn't convinced that a long session was necessary. I looked for an excuse to cancel all week long and I was really agitated the day of the appointment, but I did show up. During the first hour I lay silent in a fetal position on the couch without saying a word but I was seething inside. When I finally did speak, I was a swearing hot mess. It was like my father walked in the room and I let him have it.

I was through trying to explain his behaviors to anyone; he was a selfish bastard. I was glad he was dead. And then I told him that he had left me when I needed him most and I missed him. I explained that just when I was screwing up my courage to do life; he had signaled that it wasn't worth it. I screamed at him for leaving Mom without a partner after she had been so good to him. I blamed him for all the anguish and depression in my heart. I raged and spewed on. I emptied myself of years of disappointment, loss, heartache, pretense, and questions.

Finally, I was spent, and I cried one of the great cleansing cries of my life. Afterwards, I was lighter. And then I said "I'm sorry Dad, forgive me. I forgive you!" What a moment! I can still feel the power of that forgiveness as I write this…wow!!!

The trouble with alcoholics is that everything that has to do with them seems written in water. It is hard to remember what they were before they were an alcoholic. I was the self-appointed keeper of my father's memory and his was a wavy image at best. I have two photos of him; one in his navy uniform, and he was beautiful. I loved that picture. And then there was this horrible photo he had someone take of him shortly before he died. It was an awful a wasted face, blank and lifeless really. His eyes were cold and he had an expression that seemed to say "Yah? So what?"

I hated that picture; it was too true I guess and I think he left it as a testament to his hopelessness. But there I was caught between a romantic image of a young sailor off for adventure and an old salt beaten by life and weary of his own breath. It was interesting that shortly after my "long session" a cousin of mine sent me a picture of my dad at her wedding. He was tending bar, looking at the camera with confidence and swagger and I liked that image.

It seemed to capture the real man that was lost down the battle of alcoholism and depression; he was my dad.

I have that image now of him always and it comforts me. In recovering myself I have found that I have recovered my father as well. The process is so worth it and it continues to this day. I am so thankful; there is an old song that says" I wouldn't take nothing for my journey now!" That is exactly how I feel.

With everything that can happen to a child in their early experiences, my situation seems so miniscule and innocuous. I wasn't beaten, raped verbally abused. I wasn't starved or held captive in a closet. I don't know how devastating those experiences can be. But the result is the same the incursion of SHAME in a person's life a sense of powerless and worthlessness at the core of your being which reinforces the inner person.

QUESTIONS

Using the title of this chapter is, "My Story… Everyone Has One," write your story using power words to describe your journey.

How have those experiences resulted in the incursion of shame in your life? Name as many as you can.

In what ways have you "polished the apple" of your own story to minimize having to face the truth?

CHAPTER ELEVEN: FATHERLESSNESS – ATTEMPTING LIFE WITHOUT COVERING OR BLESSING

"Without real authority and leadership in the home, a void will be created and IT WILL BE FILLED. Without a Father's influence that covering will be found elsewhere and the ELSEWHERE does not bode well for our culture or the world at large. FATHERLESSNESS HAS A HUGE COST, emotionally, financially, and sociologically. Fatherlessness is a core issue and a major source of personal and cultural unrest and chaos"
Kathryn Murray

Many times, while serving on prayer lines, and ordinary conversation I see a pattern repeated over and over; a theme which is like a cancer on self-esteem. It reveals a sense of powerlessness and a lack of confidence, and it is this: the increasing and pervasive state of FATHERLESSNESS in our culture.

It is pervasive, and has now begun to appear as the status quo.

Our American culture has since the 60's and the woman's liberation movement slowly eroded the importance of men in their most important role as husband and father.

There are very few cultural icons that position men in a favorable light; they are seen as perpetual adolescents (the Hang Over series) as incompetent fathers (Homer Simpson Two and a Half MEN) or as randy pleasure seekers leaving children and wives and responsibility in the wake of pursuing their urgencies and personal ambition and drive (Mad Men, The Good Wife) or just plain silly and of no consequence (Family Guy, Peter Griffin).

Popular entertainment reflects the current culture, and redefines and educates the population; I believe there is a distinct agenda on the part of the cultural gurus, king-makers, and entertainment producers, and that agenda does not promote what is labeled and often derided as "traditional values."

The media and entertainment have a homogenizing effect on our culture, and creates an in-step mindset without us really being critically aware (or desiring to be) of the agenda or its effects and that influence is intentional and aggressive. It is pervasive and all-encompassing, and it unwittingly conforms all of us. The affect is to make us believe that this is the new status quo. Personally, I am utterly blown away by the affects this new normal is having on the country I have grown up in; it is like I have disappeared down one of Alice's rabbit holes. Barely any part of my country, or the culture I grew up in, is accessible today; the rabbit hole and its strange potions and distortions have become the "new reality." Good luck waking up from the dream; it is the reality and it is working a serious disengagement from valuable and time-tested ways of managing and defining life.

In critical areas like personal responsibility, family formation and our belief systems and the change is not good in my opinion and there are real consequences that have been ushered in with all these redefinitions.

THE PERVASIVE CONDITION OF FATHERLESSNESS IN OUR CULTURE IS ONE OF THEM.

In many cultures there are rituals that help young men define themselves as adults and fully responsible members of the culture in to which they are born and by performing these tasks, quests, and culturally defined rituals the young men are given status and acceptance. We have few such rituals in our culture; perhaps obtaining a driver's license and graduating high school and turning 21 suffice as our rite of passage.

In many cultures, there is also an emphasis on the importance of the FATHER'S BLESSING. In the Jewish culture it was a very valuable thing; it carried wealth and position and was revered and valued. There are many scenes depicted in the Bible of a patriarch passing his blessing on to the next generation.

The blessing business was serious business.

OBTAINING THE FATHER'S BLESSING ASSURED YOU OF STATUS WITHIN YOUR COMMUNITY.

It was a key to success and self-understanding and without it you were naked and vulnerable. In our culture today the absence of fathers and the influence of fathers is staggeringly obvious.

Without role models to show young men what it means to be a man; a lot of young men find themselves with the uneasy and now fragile task of defining manhood themselves and though their peer group. It is Lord of the Flies all over again, unfathered and vulnerable children forced to make their own rules in a cultural dessert without rules and signposts or examples.

Fatherlessness has long been a feature of the American Black culture and there are many reasons for this, I realize, I am not a racist I am simply stating a definable and researchable fact of sociology. American Black culture has been in many ways a matriarchal society with men on the periphery of normal family life. And the result has been disastrous; because of the absence of a legitimate male authority in the home the gang model has stepped in to help young men struggling with identity find a role model in gang life.

The gang is for all intensive purposes a surrogate family whose rules supersede the rules of the natural home. And what do get there as a definition of manhood; violence, an abuse of women and a degrading of their purpose and the upgrading of sex and creating babies as a rite of passage the proof that you are a real man. And the cycle repeats itself…more babies raised by mothers without the influence of a father in the house.

The whole Hip-Hop culture reflects these street creds and they are reinforced in the popular culture. Have you ever asked yourself why Hip-Hop culture is so popular with young white men these days? Well one answer is really simple to me; it is because the white culture in this country is also affected by the pall of FATHERLESSNESS.

Our culture now produces 43 percent of its children into single parent, predominantly female homes. So, the young men being raised in those homes are also feeling the effects of missing fathers as effective role models. Little wonder why they are attracted to the Hip-Hop culture; it speaks the language of alienation, anger and empowerment through violence, sexual exploits, and a pervasive hatred of authority. But these same young men could just as easily be attracted to White Supremacy groups who give easy answers to the difficult problems associated attaining a real sense of self, maturity, and acceptance in our current culture.

Without real authority and leadership in the home a void will be created and it will be filled. It is a fundamental need in us to belong, to find a place, to matter and to be covered and protected. That covering and protection was designed to be given by the father's influence in the home.

WITHOUT A FATHER'S INFLUENCE THAT COVERING WILL BE FOUND ELSEWHWERE.

The "elsewhere" does not bode well for the future of our culture. The statistics are alarming: children living in single parent households are more likely to live in poverty, abuse drugs, do poorly in school, have behavior issues and have greater rate of incarceration as an adult...wow!

FATHERLESSNESS HAS A HUGE COST: EMOTIONALLY, FINANCIALLY AND SOCIOLOGICALY. FATHERLESSNESS IS A BIG ISSUE AND A MAJOR SOURCE OF PERSONAL AND CULTURAL UNREST AND CHAOS.

Since I have the advantage of six decades of observation. I can see the effects of fatherlessness in a very real way reflected in five generations of relations. I can reach back in memory over a century within the memory back to grandparents, long gone and a whole generation that has gone before me of aunts and uncles.

I was amazed recently while tending my parent's grave on Memorial Day that my father would have been 96 and my mother 90. That means that my perspective extends more than 100 years back...whew! I know that while the marriages of my ancestors were far from perfect the unions remained intact. Good bad or indifferent there was a father in the house. In my parents' generation 12 individuals on both sides there was only one divorce (11 percent of the population group) and that was a state secret no one ever talked about it.

The stories of those families are not always heartwarming or graceful but their marriage survived all the mess. I can't account for all the cousins produced from those original 12...there were a lot of them, but as for my immediate family, the four girls only I am divorced (25 per cent of the population group) but interestingly of the four guys that married into our family only one of them had the influence of their original biological father in their lives (75 percent of the population group,)

That brings us to our immediate children seven in all; only one lives with his original wife. The others have three divorces among them, four if you count my son in-law. (50 percent of the population group, a little less than the national average).

But here is where it gets interesting to me, my daughter's generation has eleven children between them and only four of those children live with their biological fathers (a staggering 63 per cent of this current generation lacks daily contact with their original father) And I think this study of my immediate family serves to underscore and reflect the changes in our society as a whole. That is overwhelming to me and presents an incredible challenge for the future.

THESE ARE CHILDREN WITHOUT THE BIOLOGICAL FATHER' S COVERING OR BLESSING.

Now in our case many surrogates have stepped up to the plate to be a father to these children out of necessity and love, but has there ever been such a time in our culture and such a vacuum in the very basic materials to produce healthy personal formation and role identification?

What does a father provide in a household? Ideally; the role of protector and provider and an establisher of discipline and authority? The role model a father plays is invaluable and critical on so many levels; for example, the way a father/husband treats his spouse serves as a template for his son's treatment of women.

The way a man treats his wife also sets expectations in the lives of his daughters on how a man should treat a woman. I really think that contributes to young men making babies without any regard for the responsibilities and long-term consequences. In the recent past I had a temporary job in a warehouse that primarily employs men. After the months I had been there I was able to make a lot of observations based on the conversations I engaged in and just the random talk around the place.

There are those guys who are older and have just meet sons they fathered along the way having to answer all the questions and anger that their discarded children bring to them.

My heart goes out to these guys; they are reaping what they have sown and responsibility that they have avoided is pounding on their door. On the opposite side of the spectrum, it is interesting how angry some to the younger guys are because they are being forced to pay child support. It is as if their making a baby with someone is the end of the conversation and the end of their involvement. When the court system steps in to assess liability and declares otherwise a lot of the men are not happy; they feel unfairly trapped into an obligation. My point is; this now is common for the

Legal system to have to be an arbitrator of responsibility that would have been so obvious a few decades ago; namely, that you are responsible for your child. But when many of these people were never cared for, protected, or given a role model to educate and mold them; they are drawing out of an empty account. When there hasn't been that example of protection authority and responsibility passed down to them, their ignorance is a national problem.

FATHERLESSNESS IS AN EXPENSIVE PROBLEM AND SOCIETY AT LARGE IS PAYING THE COST.

I can say personally that I understand the power of the "Father's blessing." I was the favored child of my father and always felt that he saw me, appreciated my talents, and encouraged me to pursue my talents and gifting. I felt that he was proud of me.

Chaos Eaters

I felt I had his blessing whether I deserved it or not. I cannot speak directly for my sisters but in our conversations and interactions over the years; I think don't think that had that same sense of blessing.

They feel that in our family, I had gotten the lions' share of my father's attention and love. It has affected our relationship over the years and how could it not. Our household was dysfunctional; my father was a functional alcoholic until he wasn't able to function. The last years of his life were very sad and two of sisters were left to pick up the pieces. That could never have felt fair to them. I really had received so much of the family's limited resources at the time. I was in college, the first girl in the family to have ever gone to college but I had picked an expensive Catholic all girls' college to go to and so a lot of resources in the family were earmarked for my education.

One of my sisters talked about having only two dresses for her high school years and whenever she would ask for anything the standard response was," we are putting your sister through college." Privileged me lived unaware of the sacrifice everyone was making on my behalf.

That is the privilege of "the father's blessing" it comes to you often because you are first and there really isn't anything fair about it all, but its benefits are real and I have walked in a confidence in my life and a sense my own ability to succeed.

All my sisters are overcomers of an alcoholic home and I did not pay the dearest price to care for my dad in his last desperate days. I was away already in California stretching my wings.

His suicide was a real hurt to all of us which we recover from in pieces, as individuals and as a group. But we all had a different experience of Dad and I am convinced I got the best of it…not fair at all…but that is truth.

I didn't know about the benefits of the "father's blessing" until much later in my life but I have always felt I had it and I am glad for it. These days almost no one receives that blessing through the result of formation of single-family homes, divorce and remarriage and the dynamics of blended families. And the absence of blessing invites a curse; something enters the void and creates a generation that is searching for acceptance and approval and a place of belonging often in the wrong places and more and more often with disastrous implications for individuals, families, and the larger culture.

Every generation requires individuals and rituals that will form a bridge for the new generation to walk over into a responsible and life affirming next stage. And I am afraid that so many are parenting today that have had neither the example or the experience of being welcomed into the adult world and are parenting the next generation with a very immature and stunted understanding of what used to be rather common values. We are a culture without elders and we are suffering for it.

I have memories of certain people in my life that recognized me and invited to the adult's table. Remember the day at family gatherings that you graduated from the "kid's table" and sat with the adolescents and teen-agers. That was a good day; you felt you were making progress, growing up and there was a place reserved for you. Increasingly this simple ritual and the more profound ones are absent from the fabric of modern life.

Chaos Eaters

Families are more and more disjointed and immaturity runs up and down the group from the sons to the fathers (if they are present) to the increasing matriarchal structure of our homes. There are less and less bridges to cross and fewer and fewer examples to follow and there is chaos in our society because of it. I was blessed in my Father's love for me. He was a flawed man, as all men are, but I realize more and more that I had his blessing. He was proud of me and he enjoyed my company and my thoughts. He thought I was brilliant and because of that I thought I was.

My sisters have a different view of my father largely because of the increasingly debilitating effects of alcoholism. I may have got the best of him; I can't apologize for that. I am thankful for it; it has made a great difference in my life. I know the power of the father's blessing. I have received it. I also had other important people in my life invite me over to the adult world at very crucial moments.

For example, I had an Aunt Irene a very flamboyant, colorful, independent, and feisty gal who really liked me. At her funeral I told a story about one morning up at her cabin in Northern Minnesota. Every morning, my aunt used to get up early and head into Crosslake to get fresh bakery goods. I realize now that I am older that it was her private time. The time where she could just relax and be herself before the demands of the day kicked in.

Knowing that now makes what she did for me all the more remarkable because one morning she invited me along. She woke me up, told me to hurry and get dressed because I was going to go with her to the bakery.

I was excited. I felt very grown up and special to be asked to go with her. On the way there, she didn't ignore me or ride in silence she asked questions and was interested in my response; a heady thing for a young girl in the throes of awkward adolescence. It was a wonderful morning.

When we got to the bakery, my aunt greeted the woman behind the counter like an old friend. I saw that this moment in both their days was special to each of them and I felt special to be invited in. I was able to pick my own pastry, a long john, I recall. And when I was asked what I wanted to drink, I paused for a moment and said "coffee." I had never had coffee before but they were drinking it along with their cigarettes and I thought I should drink coffee too, as one of the "girls." I didn't think to ask for a cigarette but asking for coffee made me feel real, grown up. I remember my aunt laughed and said "Coffee, are you sure?" I shook my head. "Okay, coffee it is, but make sure you put lots of cream in it." So, there I was eating my pastry and drinking coffee with the gals. What a moment!

Why was it so important and why do I remember the morning even to this day? Someone held out a bridge and invited me to come across. I remember telling that story at her funeral and out in the audience there were so many knowing smiles. I realized that I wasn't the only one that had that experience with my aunt; those faces out there knew what I was talking about. Now that is legacy and the older, I get, the more I want to invite younger people across the bridge.

There are so few people equipped to do that these days. I have received such kindness and attention and it is my heart to do the same for others.

And that is sorely lacking our culture, we are too busy or too ill-equipped to serve in this way and we are suffering for the loss of such moments.

Look at these statistics on a Fatherless America.

A Myriad of maladies: fatherless children are at dramatically greater risk of drug and alcohol abuse, mental illness, suicide, poor educational performance, teen pregnancies and criminality.

Source: US Dept. of Health and Human Resources, Survey on Child Health

Sexual Abuse: A study of child sexual abuse victims found that the majority of the children came from disrupted or single-parent homes, only 31 percent of the children surveyed lived with both biological parents. Although stepfamilies made up only 10 percent of the survey of all families 27 percent of abused children lived either with a stepfather or the mother's boyfriend. Source:

Beverly Gomes-Schwartz, Jonathan Schwartz, "Child Sexual Abuse," US Dept. of Justice, Office of Juvenile Justice.

High Risk: According to a study of adolescent suicide victims, teens living in single parent homes are not only more likely to commit suicide but also are more likely to suffer from psychological disorders, when compared to teens living in intact families.

Source: David A Brent, "Post Traumatic Stress Disorders in Peers of Adolescent Suicide Victims" Journal of the American Academy of Child and Adolescent Psychiatry 34.

Confused Identities: Boys who grow-up in father-absent homes are more likely than those in father present homes to have trouble establishing appropriate sex roles and gender identity.

Source: P.L. Adams, J.R. Milner, and N.A. Scherff, Fatherless Children, New York, Wiley Press.

Psychiatric Problems: In a study of pre-school children admitted to New Orleans hospitals as psychiatric patients over a thirty-four-month period found that nearly 80 percent came from fatherless homes.

Source: Jack Block ET all "Parental Functioning and the Home Environment in Families of Divorce" Journal of the American Academy of Child and Adolescent Psychiatry, 27.

Uncooperative Kids: Children reared by a divorced or never-married mother are less cooperative and score lower on tests of intelligence than children reared in intact families. Statistical analysis of the behavior and intelligence of these children revealed "significant detrimental effects" of living in a female-headed household. Growing up in a female-headed household remained a statistical predictor of behavior problems even after adjusting for differences in family income.

Source: Greg L. Duncan, Jeanne Brooks-Gunn, and Pamela Kato Klebanov. "Economic Deprivation and Early Childhood Deelopment"65.

Unstable Families, Unstable Lives: Compared to peers in two-parent homes, black children in single parent households are more likely to engage in troublesome behavior and perform poorly in school.

Source: Tom Luster and Harriette Pipes McAdoo, "Factors Related to the Achievement and Adjustment of Young African American Children" Child Development 65.

Troubled Marriage, Troubled Kids: Compared to peers living with both biological parents, sons, and problems. Daughters of divorce parents or separated parents exhibited significantly more conduct Daughters of divorced or separated mothers evidenced significantly higher rates of internalizing problems, such as anxiety or depression.

Source: Denise B. Kandel, Emily Rosen Baum and Kevin Chen, "Impact of Maternal Drug Use and Life Experiences on Preadolescent Children Born to Teenage Mothers>" Journal of Marriage and Family, 56.

Fatherless Aggression: In a longitudinal study of 1,197 fourth grade students' researchers observed "greater levels of aggression" in boys from mother-only households than from boys in father mother households.

Source. Vaden-Kierman, N. Ialongo, J. Pearson and S. Kellam,"Household Family Structure and Children's Aggressive Behavior; A longitudinal Study of Urban Elementary School Children". Journal of abnormal Child Psychology 23, no 5.

Expelled: Nationally, 15.3 percent of children living with a never-married mother and 10.7 percent of children living with a divorce mother have been expelled or suspended from school, compared to only 4.4 percent form children living with both biological parents.

Source: Debra Dawson, "Family Structure..." Journal of Marriage and Family, no 53.

Dad less Dropouts: After taking into account race, socio-economic status, sex, age, and ability high school students from single –parent households are 1.7 times more likely to drop out than were their Corresponding counterparts living with both biological parents.

Source; Ralph McNeal, Sociology of Education, 88.

Rearing Rapists: Seventy-two percent of adolescent murderers grew up without fathers. Sixty percent of America's rapists grew up the same way.

Source: Behavioral Science and the Law,5.

Count 'Em.: Seventy percent of juveniles in the state reform institutions grew up in single or no-parent situations.

Source: Alan Beck, et all, "Survey of Youth in Custody," UCSC Bureau of Justice Statistics.

QUESTIONS

What voids were created because of a lack of leadership (fatherlessness) in your home?

Describe how you did not (or did) receive your BIOLOGICAL FATHER' S COVERING OR BLESSING.

If you did not receive your biological father's covering or blessing, who stepped in as a surrogate? If no one did, how has that impacted your life?

CHAPTER TWELVE: WHAT IS, IS; WHAT ISN'T, ISN'T!

"So, it is always a good idea to ask ourselves what fantasies we are funding to avoid clearly seeing the truth of a situation which is untenable"
Kathryn Murray

Funny little statement isn't? What is, is! What isn't, isn't!

I spent twenty-four years in the Financial Services Industry and as a result I went to countless training sessions expected to improve performance in our business model. Some of those sessions were downright silly, but many presentations have made their way into the bed rock of my life; ideas that made so much sense that I have applied them to my life over and over again with great and positive affect.

Probably chief among them was the teaching: "What is, is! What isn't, isn't!" You really have to put your head around that little statement to catch the meaning. It is a worthwhile task because when you do; light bulbs go off and a revelation of the real way of things is a result.

I have found in my own life and in the lives of others that so much of our turmoil and chaos comes because we do not accurately assess the life situations, problems, and circumstances in our lives. So many of us rationalize and fantasize our circumstances and always try to make something that is into something that isn't.

Or, we've tried to make something that will never be, and make it into something that is.

The Bible says that hope differed makes the heart sick. Real clarity and understanding are achieved only when we really allow ourselves to see a circumstance without factoring in our wishes, hopes, fantasies and magic thinking and come to accept the situation, relationship, struggle, or problem AS IT REALLY IS NOT THE WAY WE WANT IT TO BE.

This is the first step before any real change can occur. Addicts know this they must first declare that they have a problem before they can solve a problem, if they cover, excuse, and assess blame on others they have no real chance of recovery. And conversely, those who have to deal with addicted and dysfunctional behaviors cannot really make progress in working out the situation until they get away from making excuses and their false hopes for a change.

Before changes can happen there must be a revelation of the real issues (the what is) without that there is no hope for remedy. Still, individuals can live their whole lives without reconciling with their past and dragging the effects of dysfunction into every new situation. They cope with real problem by fantasizing, wishing' and hoping," so to speak.

So much dis-ease and chaos because we are not the right dress size and weight, live at the right address, have the right spouse, or have a spouse, the right job, the right color of skin, the right pedigree and on and on and on. The cycle of disappointment and false comparison. That cycle will kill any nurturing of peace and wholeness in your life. Why?

It is because you are constantly focusing on what you lack instead of what you have; how can peace prosper in such hyper disappointed soil. And because we tend to be so outwardly focused in these comparisons, we leave our real gifting and talents neglected and left to atrophy.

I will illustrate with a family story about an infamous aunt in my family, "M." "M" was a size 18-20 for most of the time I knew her and but if you had checked her closet you would have found racks of clothing in sizes 10 and 12 with the tags still on them because none of them fit her. The really sad part of the story was that she got herself in heaps of debt funding her fantasy wardrobe and it caused a lot of friction in her marriage until she circumvented the issue by having those bills come to a post office box leaving her husband in the dark about her indebtedness.

That is like all of us refusing the "what is" in our lives; we fund fantasies and create havoc in our worlds. So, it is always a good question to ask ourselves what fantasies we are funding to avoid the truth of a situation which is untenable.

What we hide from ourselves and others will cost us. The basis of those situations is a lie which we are trying to pervert into a crippled and ineffective truth to suit our brokenness and attachment to a false idea of who we are. By avoiding the tough questions in our lives regarding our attachments and fantasies, we leave our real life promises and gifting unopened, unappreciated, and unused…we lose our real selves in the pursuit of a fantasy. What is, TRULY is! And what isn't, REALLY isn't!

What is the significance of embracing this as truth?

You are finally able to excavate the lies that have covered your idea of who you are and begin to unwind the dead things that have attached themselves to the false sense of identity. That will include relationships, ways of behaving and coping with past hurts and grievances. Truth will begin to shed light into dark spaces that you have held closed, boarded up and locked. We are all in bondage because of fear and misguided attempts to negotiate with your pain by avoiding i.e., spend our time filling our insecurity and emptiness with things, people, activities, and ideas which do not satisfy precisely because they are based on a lie. Painful, sure? Difficult? You bet! Worthwhile? Oh absolutely!

Why? Because you can finally come home and find an authentic self with real talents and preferences and gifting. I will illustrate this point with a story from own life. I was close to my father as I have said in my story, but he was troubled; an alcoholic and he finally died a suicide from the final effects of his addiction. I did not like his story, or his ending and for years with really being aware of what I was doing I would ascribe any witty and bright thing I said to my father. I would always preface those remarks with "As my father used to say…" what was I trying to do by that? Well, it is clear to me now; I was a revisionist and wanted to keep changing the image of my father by ascribing my bright, witty, and funny thoughts and words to him.

I guess I felt that but polishing the apple of his reputation. I was revising his story and making his life choices and death more acceptable. Was I aware that was my intention? Not at the time, but if I kept this fantasy going, I couldn't really deal with my father's real influence in my life or fully process the devastation of his passing.

Building and maintaining a façade is a tough and unsatisfying business. The energy we spend (that I spent) promoting my fantasy idea of my father kept me from honoring and accepting my own gifts and talents; and accepting and being grateful for his real influence in my life. As I type these words on the page I am smiling because he really did infuse me with a love for words and the printed page, so I know that my writing would please him.

That is a real understanding of our relationship and is so much better then promoting a fantasy... because it is WHAT IS! Not what I wanted it to be; there is real peace and comfort in that.

QUESTIONS

Describe what it means to say: "What is, is! What isn't, isn't!"

Where have you rationalized or fantasized your circumstances. How have you tried to make something that is into something that isn't?

Take a moment now and write down what you believe the real issue, or issues are. Write down at least one.

What "fantasies" have you funded in your life? How have they created havoc in your world?

CHAPTER THIRTEEN: UNKNOWN, RED LIGHT, GREEN LIGHT, AND FLASHING YELLOW

"I have come to categorize my relationships into four categories: unknown, green light, red light and flashing yellow."
Kathryn Murray

I have come to categorize my relationships into four categories: Unknown, Green Light, Red Light and Flashing Yellow. Let me explain what I mean by that. The Unknowns are exactly that; unknown. These are people that I haven't had enough interaction with to understand their preferences and perspectives. I generally try to give these people a compassionate eye. After all, I do not know them at all and my first interaction because of my personality is generally to try to make them like me.

I have learned that some people remarkably, do not like me and I have learned to be okay with that. But in my initial encounter with almost anyone I meet I give them the benefit of the doubt. With people that you do know however, they tend to break down into three categories.

The "Green Light People" are always ready to receive you. They receive you with delight and seek your company and wish you well. They will encourage you, support you and carry you when you are down. Because of the years of interactions, you can approach them without any shield of guardedness. You have learned that you can trust them; they are for you. The second category that is definite is the Red-Light individuals of your acquaintance.

These people have made it very clear that you are never going to be the apple of their eye, or their cup of tea. It isn't hard to know how to act around these people, because as open as you can be with the Green Light People in your life; you are forced to be closed to the "Red Light People."

To present your vulnerable underbelly to Red Lighters is to invite serious emotional and even physical injury. They are not for you and are often adversarial and often will actively seek you harm. It isn't hard to see why you don't disclose anything of value to them; they would trample it underfoot and use it as a weapon to reinforce their negative opinion of you to themselves and others.

When forced to be in contact with them it is best to be very wary of what you say and do around them. I find that I am best off with very limited exposure to people who are my enemies; but sometimes contact cannot be avoided and I am wise to be on my guard. It is futile to keep trying to persuade such individuals in your life that they are wrong about you. It is hard to open a closed door and to keep knocking to gain an entrance denied to you is to invite disdain and a sense of rejection and chaos not to mention bruised knuckles. And don't keep asking them for permission to move ahead they have made it their business to stop you from being anything but their idea of you.

It is pretty clear that the Green Lighters and the Red Lighters in your life are the easiest to sort out. The tricky people are those I call "Flashing Yellow People." Why are they so difficult? Because you never know what the reaction is going to be when you enter into an intersection with them.

Chaos Eaters

One day they are positive and welcoming and the next day indifferent and cold. You can never really know what to expect. You can never anticipate what their reception is going to be based on past interactions.

There is a lot of confusion in dealing with such people. And there is a temptation to second guess yourself. You wonder what you did wrong or conversely, what you did right. There really is no rhyme or reason for their actions toward you. So, for our own peace of mind, just count the good encounters as positive but never get fooled into thinking it is the new normal, because it generally isn't.

QUESTIONS

Using what you learned in this chapter, identify whether the key people in your life are Unknown, Green Light, Red Light, or Flashing Yellow.

How have you second guessed those people in your life? In what ways has that stopped you, or held you back?

CHAPTER FOURTEEN: WITHOUT *REVELATION WE ARE UNRESTRAINED*

"Fortunately, for us, there is in each of us what St. Francis called "a God-shaped hole that only God can fill. "Now, in our hurt, pain, shame, rejection, abandonment, abuse and hopelessness we have attempted to stuff a lot of junk into that hole. Drugs, alcoholic, careless living; success, unworthy relationships, sex, food, religion, fanaticism; rage hatred, pessimism, and despair. And what has been the end result of all of these efforts? More darkness, more emptiness, more isolation, more heartache, shackles and regret; there has been more confusion and less hope and more despair...in short, more chaos!"
Kathryn Murray

There are a lot of factors that contribute to the seemingly insatiable appetite for Chaos and the purposeful disruption in our lives. The bottom line in all of this is one of perspective. If we are simply a result of organic chemistry and evolution than any way, we live our life must be seen as legitimate.

After all, if all that we call life is reduced to biology, synapses, and random acts of nature we really are not responsible for our actions. Nor can we aspire to a higher understanding of purpose, morality and the whole myth of self-improvement is a myth. And the many conventional restraints that society has placed upon its society for the mutual good must be deconstructed... Just what is the mutual good, anyway?

If we are merely organisms acting out of a chemical-swamp DNA who is to judge anyone? A long, long time ago, I remember reading Zen and the Art of Motor Cycle Mechanics. In the book, as I remember the protagonist was presented with the philosophical notion of QUALITY and it shut him down. Why worry about QUALITY or morality or righteous if we are all only a product of biology.

What would the notion of QUALITY mean? That certain conducts and understandings produce more QUALITY in a person's life? Who decided the definition of Quality anyway if we are all acting out of our own individual and personal constructs? How can we decide what a QUALITY life is? And how can we audaciously apply our constructs to anyone else? Why do we even have laws and criteria for right conduct…if everyone's definition of QUALITY is personal?

How can any standard be applied to society as a whole? Isn't that arbitrary and limiting of human potential. Ah! Human potential…just what is that when we are just glorified amphibians or an evolved ape…who cares about our potential…isn't evolution inexorably in charge of how far we can drag ourselves from the primal ooze? Why all of our efforts to understand the meaning of things… to reach our "potential"? Why should we even care about our conduct and how can we possibly judge the conduct of others?

I guess their QUALITY must be okay even as our QUALITY is; the classic "I am okay and you are okay" philosophy. I do my thing you do yours; I won't judge you don't you judge me.

Chaos Eaters

The scripture says very clearly in Proverbs 29:18 "Without REVELATION the people
Throw off restraint" (which incidentally leads to chaos). What is that "REVELATION"?

It is the polar opposite of the prevailing view of evolution and the tyranny of biology. It is this; the creation and every creature in it, is created with loving purpose and graceful intention by a God. A God who is available, approachable, and willing to reveal Himself to his creation. This revelation defines purpose and gives meaning to seemingly random events and a futile view which says essentially; you are born, you live and you die.

Why anyone with that world view ever ask about purpose, quality and potential; it is all futile anyway. But that is the REVELATION and without understanding that we are created beings we have no criteria outside of our own thoughts, education, and experience to judge anything correctly.

If we are the judge and mediator anything, we declare to be true is true and there is no absolute truth anywhere…it is always truth as we define it.

I have had many opportunities to minister in women's prisons both here in the states and in Mexico. Certainly, incarcerated people have hit the wall of conventional wisdom and conduct in the pursuit of their definition of QUALITY of life. The court system has codified a definition of acceptable conduct which limits self-expression and reaching for self-determined potential.

If you aspire to be the best thief, drug dealer, murderer or con-artist; the system will thwart your potential and we as a society determine that by limiting your self-expression and pursuit of your goals; if we determine we do this to improve the QUALITY of life for society as a whole.

No matter what drives you to fulfill your potential there are constraints written into the legal system which will limit your pursuit of your goals. I see that as many of the women realize that they had very clearly put themselves in the center of their lives…they will admit that they were the god of their little world and declared its purpose with zeal, enthusiasm, and disregard for the wellbeing of anyone else.

Then they hit the court system which judged them by their actions and put them in prison where everything is regulated and regimented. Their pursuit of their freedom cost them their liberty. Very sobering, isn't? And many of them would tell you it was the best thing that ever happened to them.

Why? Because it taught then that there were consequences to their actions and it quickly taught them that they were not as god-like as they wanted to appear. Incarceration gives them time to reassess, re-evaluate and examine QUALITY on a daily basis. Most of the ladies I minster to have discovered the FIRST PRINCIPLES that our society has disregarded, in its rush to be tolerant and embracing.

The first principal being "There is a God and He is not you!" THAT IS THE REVELATION THAT CHANGES EVERYTHING!

Chaos Eaters

Without it we as individuals and as a society are adrift on a sea of opinion, conjecture, biology, neuro-science and misplaced hope; we have no hope of overcoming the circumstances of our birth, the challenge of our regrets and mistakes, the tyranny of our life choices and the consequences inherent in them.

We are driven by our sense of loss and disconnection to an endless pursuit of things, people, and experiences to fill the void in us. It leads us to hard places and then accuses us of being in hard places; we always feel trapped and have a very careless attitude to our own well-being and that of others. All of that is certainly a recipe for feeding the Chaos in our lives. Why would it not? If all we have is our own poor selves to rely on, our own broken past, disappointments, and failures. With only yourself as a yardstick life is a long, hard go.

There is a Greek myth about a character named Sisyphus that really illustrates our human condition without REVELATION. Sisyphus was a man condemned by the gods to constantly roll a huge boulder up a mountain. Each time, just as he reached the peak, the boulder would roll back down to the base of the mountain. That was his fate; hard work, futile work then false hope and failure and then a return to his futile efforts, and wearier with every attempt.

I know I felt that way before REVELATION came to me. I was so tired of my own efforts and the lack of success and the dashed hopes and the growing fears that I contemplated suicide. I have referred in this book the effect of my father's suicide on my family's life and on my own life as well; getting to that place was a lot like incarceration; I saw no way out.

I was weary tired in my own way and yet proud and unyielding. But God uses these prisons as a place of REVELATION and renewal….so complete a change that the bible talks about as a "new-birth."

Here are the first things:

Gen.1:1 IN THE BEGINNING GOD!

That understanding, REVELATION is the first principal in overcoming Chaos and self- destruction. In the first book of the Bible, we see a picture of the Spirit of God moving over world that was without form and void and causing order and definition and meaning to manifest; divine order and purpose which was absent without divine intervention.

That is a wonderful picture of any life that allows the REVELATION of God's eternal plan and purpose into their lives; which are also without form and void; often filled with chaos and self-loathing and darkness. Our society has been quick to push the notion of a Creator out of the dialog but as I and many others have found out there is no way that can be done…" God is dead! "–Nietzsche…" Nietzsche is dead!"-God.

Not only is God not dead; He is alive, active, and seeking the best purpose and QUALITY OF LIFE FOR EACH ONE OF US. But true purpose and meaning cannot be achieved by our efforts alone; we need God. We need to recognize the power of the FATHER/CREATOR. Scripture says" the fool has said in his heart there is no God."

But the REVELATION of a loving, purposeful, and gracious God is the beginning of wisdom.

We need to know that God is for us. He is not mad. He is loving and kind and wants to reveal His heart and His personal plan for each of His children. He understands our hurts and disappointments and brokenness our shame, rejection, hurt, pain, and misery. He also understands the search for significance QUALITY of life and meaning; He put that in our heart to draw us to Him. We belong to Him not to ourselves and we need to find HIM, though in truth He is not far from any of us. THAT IS THE FIRST REVELATION.

And the second is this: JESUS IS GOD'S SON.

John1:1
In the beginning was the WORD (Jesus) and the WORD was with God and the WORD was God. The same was in the beginning with God; all things were made by Him and without Him was not anything made that was made. In Him (Jesus) was LIFE and Light and the
LIFE was the LIGHT of men. And the LIGHT shined into the darkness and the darkness comprehended it not. That was the true LIGHT which lights everyman that comes into the world. He was in the world and the world was made by HIM and the world knew HIM not. But as many as received HIM, to them HE gave the power to become the sons of God, even them who believe in His NAME.

As we receive the FATHER, we must receive the SON because He was sent to us to reveal the love of the FATHER and the great lengths that the Father would go to expose His great love for us. One of the most familiar passages of scripture is

John 3: 16
For GOD so loved the world the world that HE sent HIS SON (Jesus) that whosoever believes in HIM will not perish but have eternal life.

So, He is here this SON, this LIGHT, and this LIFE; so why don't we get it? Why didn't we understand sooner? Many of us marvel at the blindness we had before the REVELATION of GOD AND HIS SON. We wonder why we didn't get it earlier why did we pursue our wrong thinking and brokenness; we shouldn't wonder …BECAUSE DARKNESS DOESN'T GET IT! AND AS LONG AS WE WERE IN DARKNESS, WE DID NOT GET IT EITHER!

What is in the darkness? What is the darkness today?

Abuse. Drug addiction. Political intrigue and unrest, wars and rumors of wars, recessions, scandal murder, lawlessness, people living without natural affection, fatherless children…all of that and more…CHAOS FOR SURE. And under the surface of all that we have emotional and soul foundations which from as platforms to run a program of self-abuse, despair, and hopelessness.

The early child hood traumas we have discussed in this book. The places where the adults the ones in charge failed their responsibilities and God-given duties to protect nurture and provide for their children. Where the message given to children very early on is one of SHAME. That they are broken and unworthy of love and purpose and hope for a good life. That they are a product of circumstances and a perennial victim in an unchanging cycle of abuse and lack of regard and any hope for love or change or a future.

Chaos Eaters

That is the voice of darkness…the lonely struggle up the mountain pushing the rock of our life without any hope of success.

Then there is the trap of UNFORGIVENESS which has taken the bait of offense as we have discussed in other areas of this book. That unforgiveness has become a jailor as effective and vigilant as any we could have in incarceration.

Until we understand the glory of grace and forgiveness revealed in CHRIST, we sit in our emotional prisons shackled our past hurts and acting out of our abused sense of fairness and self-righteousness in every area of our lives…spreading bitterness and hopeless into every area of our lives.

That is a bitter harvest which springs up everywhere in our lives.

THIS IS DARKNESS AND IT DOESN'T GET THE LIGHT BUT NONE THE LESS LIGHT HAS COME AND HE KNOWS HIS BUISNESS.

If our way out of the darkness depended on our own puny light, we would spend all our days in cave thinking we caught glimpses of the sun.

Fortunately for us there is in each of us what St. Francis called "a God-shaped hole, which only God can fill."

Now in our hurt, pain, shame. Rejection, abandonment abuse and hopelessness we have attempted to stuff a lot of things into that hole; drugs, success, unworthy partners, sex, and food. Religion, fanaticism, rage and hatred, pessimism, and hopelessness; what has been the result of all our efforts? More darkness more emptiness, more heartache, more shackles more regret, less confidence, and less hope. And GOD loves us enough to bring periods into our lives.

We tend to love questions and exclamation points, commas and run on sentences but there is in the plan of God times when in our lives a period comes. It may not be as dramatic as a prison sentence or the suicide of a loved one.

Everyone has those moments in which God wrestles with each of us to get our attention, and reveal His heart and plan and love to us. We are not always aware that this is the plan of God for us, to get our attention…to bring REVELATION.

We often fight these times by blaming others, God, our circumstances our past; we bring out our stories and declare how "unfair" all of this is. But God is not moved by our tantrums or our despair. He is moved by His love for us and his plan for our lives. He is serious about that even when we are totally clueless and uncaring, even when we hate Him.

He is unmoved by all that because He is serious about His purpose in our lives. He already knows our stories; He already has an answer for all our questions; but he has to get our attention first.

Chaos Eaters

I am reminded of a story I heard once about two poor dirt farmers down in Appalachia. One was so poor that he didn't even have a mule to plow his fields with. So, He had to ask his neighbor to borrow his mule. He neighbor agreed and carefully gave him instructions on how he should treat his prized mule. The man was careful to listen because he was desperate for the use of the mule and was prepared to do everything he was instructed to do. So, imagine his surprise when they arrived at his field to start plowing and the neighbor who owned the mule picked up a two by four and hit the mule square in the head. The farmer was confused, so his asked his neighbor." Why did you give me all the instructions about how the take care of your mule when you are going to abuse her like that??" Oh, said his neighbor, "I do want you to be good to my mule …BUT YOU HAVE TO GET HER ATTENTION FIRST!"

God is like that farmer's neighbor sometimes, I think; He wants to be good to us but He has to get our attention first.

There is a story in the Bible that as often spoke to me over the years that I have been a follower of Christ. The character Jacob is a very modern kind of a guy. He was used to getting his own way …twisting the rules and using trickery if it seemed necessary. His very name meant "deceiver." And Like most of us he learned his deceitful ways in his home; his own momma taught how to steal a blessing that rightfully belonged to his older brother. He got it but at great cost …for one thing he had to run for his live and I do not think he ever saw his mother again. But wherever he went He knew how to work circumstance to his advantage.

He has wives and cattle and sheep and goats and wealth but there was a time when Jacob had to turn himself toward home and to the wrath of his older brother.

There is a scene in the story where Jacob is on a mountain top watching the wealth, he had accumulated over the years parade below him. And Jacob was left alone on a mountain top with only a stone for a pillow. It was definitely a period in his life; a little like a cell, all by himself with God's opportunity. God took advantage of this time and came down a wrestled with Jacob; the result of that encounter changed Jacob's entire future because something of his plans a scheme died on that mountain.

He was a changed man after that encounter with God. Physically he was touched…his hip was hurt and caused him to walk with a limp. Symbolic I have thought about how he needed to learn as we all do to not lean on our own understanding but to lean on God. He was also given a new name after that encounter a name that declared God's purpose for him not his own definition of himself…Jacob, the deceiver now became Israel, a Prince with God.

Now that is every believer's story. Whatever circumstance brings us to REVELATION of God's love and FELLOWSHIP with His Son is a blessing though it is often disguised at the time. There is no darkness that can stand against that grace and understanding; nothing from your past, not your shortcomings and sin not your misguided attempts to be god in your own world…nothing. AND THAT IS HOW LIGHT OVERCOMES DARKNESS!

QUESTIONS

How have you tried to fill the "God-shaped hole" in your life?

What losses or disconnections have caused you to try to fill a void in your life with the pursuit of things, people, and experiences?

Where are the places of "darkness" in your own life?

Name some examples of times God has wrestled with you to get your attention, and reveal His heart and plan and love to you.

CHAPTER FIFTEEN: THE KINGDOM OF GOD IS NOT A KINGDOM OF CHAOS

"Sin is, in its essence, a rebellion against the authority and order of God. It is a rebellion against the first principal of the Universe and the One who created it. So, by its very nature, sin includes CHAOS. CHAOS is the natural by-product of rebelliousness. So, it stands to reason that if we walk in rebelliousness, the more CHAOS will be evident in our lives."
Kathryn Murray

From the first book in the Bible, Genesis, where the world is described as being without form and void God's voice spoke over the formless void, God's purpose and plan has been revealed in order. His design and purpose are seen in the divine order of things we see in the creation.

Chaos is always the opposite of order…the antithesis of God's plan for His creation. The more we begin the walk-in obedience to the revelation of God's order for the world and our lives personally the less chaos will have control of our lives.

Jesus says in a scripture that means so much to me personally, "Come unto me all you who labor and are heavy-laden and I will give you rest. Take my yoke upon you and learn of me, for my yoke is easy and my burden is light"

He can make those promises to those Chaos prone, burdened separated from God, because the scripture He was there with the Creator from the beginning and He is the answer to Chaos from the beginning of things.

He came to reveal the Father and the Father's order and plan to a world that had lost its way and was separated from the original design and was awash in Chaos. Chaos is the antithesis of God's design.

Jesus said that "The kingdom of God is righteousness, peace and joy in the Holy Ghost" Romans 14:17 The Kingdom of God which Jesus came to reveal did not include tumult, uproar, agitation upheaval and confusion.

Those things run contrary to the order of the Father He came to reveal. His description of the Kingdom is the yardstick that we must use when we are examining our lives in Christ. It is to the precise extent that we are walking in righteousness (able to do the right thing), peace, (being at rest even during struggles) and joy (enjoying the Presence of God which is fullness of joy) that we are in the kingdom.

If we find that our life after coming into the kingdom is still full of confusion, distress, commotion, turmoil, and strife that we must ask ourselves "What Kingdom do we think we are part of, that is not the Kingdom of God.'

The status quo is a terrible taskmaster. We can accept a life far below our privilege and calling in Christ if we do not get past our own thoughts and feelings. We need to examine the life we are living in light of the declared purposes of God in the Word.

Chaos Eaters

The purpose of God is ALWAYS ORDER. If we name the name of Jesus and still find that our lives are disordered and chaotic, we need to return to the Word and the Power of the Spirit to find the power to align more correctly with his purpose and plan for our lives.

Still, we can't judge our success or failure on the lives of others. We must find a standard in something bigger than ourselves and others. We must seek the promise of the Word and begin to ask for the strength that only God can give to line us up to His promises and purposes. That is the process of reconciliation of all things to God through Jesus Christ.

That isn't an easy process, but it is a *possible* process because of the promises of God, the love of His Son, and the power of the Holy Spirit.

However, first we must be honest with ourselves. We must ask the hard questions about how closely our lives display the righteousness, peace and joy Jesus said is the hallmark of the Kingdom and His followers. We will find that the original joy of our conversion experience does not change our character overnight and that may discourage us.

God's plan is eternal and long term as we walk with Him. The more fully we align ourselves with the word and the work of the Holy Spirit in our lives, we will find that we progressively begin to walk in more and more obedience to His order and plan for our lives. But CHAOS does not give up without a fight. We would be naïve to believe that becoming conformable to the will of God for our lives is an easy road.

In fact, we it is a supernatural task that can only be accomplished through supernatural means.

The good news is that those means have been provided: The Word, the Blood and the power of the Holy Spirit working within our lives. We will find that more we yield to the influence of these tools the easier it is to line up with the order of God. Little by little we yield more of the control of our lives unto the plan of the Original Planner.

Sin is in its essence a rebellion against the authority and order of God. It is a rebellion against the first principals of the universe and the One who created it. So, by its very nature sin includes CHAOS. CHAOS is the natural by-product and companion of rebelliousness. It only stands to reason that the more we walk in rebelliousness the more CHAOS will be in our lives.

By the same token, the more that we walk in obedience to the authority and rule of God the less CHAOS there will be in our lives. God is in Christ reconciling all things to the Father. As a Reconciler, Jesus' job is to defeat CHAOS and restore the original order and authority of God.

It is encouraging to me that the scripture says that where sin abounds, grace (Gods unmerited favor) abounds more. As we struggle to conform to God's Will for our lives and defeat our rebellious and chaotic nature, grace abounds! What a thought! In our personal struggles inherent in overcoming our sin nature, the grace and power of God is more for us.

It is encouraging to me that precisely when I feel most out of control that is the moment that the resources of heaven are the most at my disposal.

Chaos Eaters

God's word says that with every temptation He will make a way of escape; we can escape the CHAOS which wishes to throw us into upheaval, torment, confusion by escaping into the order and authority of God. We cannot defeat Chaos, or its effect on our lives on our own. And in this world, we will have troubles, Jesus said so... but He also encouraged us by saying don't worry about that, "I have overcome the world!"

In our lives, we will continually fight the good fight of faith and find that through Christ we will progressively overcome the allure and power of CHAOS but only as we submit to God's authority and rules. The path of Christian discipleship, note the root word...discipline is to Trust and obey and as we do we become more and more conformed to the will of God for our lives and the plan of God for His creation, and that not only frees us from the tyranny of CHAOS but it pleases God!

QUESTIONS

Where has chaos and confusion caused you to miss the declared purposes of God for your life?

How closely does your lives display the righteousness, peace and joy Jesus said is the hallmark of the Kingdom and His followers?

Describe how walking in obedience to the authority and rule of God impact the amount of Chaos in your life.

EPILOGUE

I was having dinner with a few wonderful friends awhile back. We had not seen each other for some time and so we spent a lovely evening over a wonderful dinner catching up on each other's lives. The topics went back and forth in a lively and supportive exchange and when the subject of my book came up my friends were eager to hear about the topics involved in such an arresting title…" The CHAOS EATERS." And the subject gravitated toward the subject of what is culturally kind of gathered under the umbrella topic of "Baggage."

It was agreed that everyone carries the weight of life's disappointments, rejections, losses and the vestiges of lost dreams and brokenness; it is accepted as part of the business of life, and many of these influences are covered in the book.

What was interesting to me however was that the consensus among my friends is that we always carry these things with us; that they are just a part of the human condition? And to an extent I agree, all of these things are a part of the human condition but where I disagree is that these things need to be an inseparable and endemic part of an individual's life.

The whole point of my book is to encourage people that they do not have to continue to act out of and be captive to those influences, hurts and past brokenness.

There is hope to overcoming what I have called CHAOS Addiction and attaining an authentic self. It is similar to the problem I have with twelve step programs because one of the underlying premises is that" once an addict always and addict" and hence, the need for maintenance programs to retain sobriety in all its aspects.

I thought about that dinner a lot and realized that the real difference in my understanding of the ongoing issue of 'Baggage' is that I have experienced the "born again "experience.

There really was a point in my life where I literally was one person going one way and carrying all the brokenness of my life on my own and failing; it almost cost me my life. And then, I was miraculously someone else learning to cast my burdens on the One who died that I could live again. I even have a date for that day of deliverance and revelation, February 3rd. 1974. Everything that I have learned about an overcoming life and the topics that I approach in my book flow out of that bedrock moment.

It was when I realized I was not alone and that there was a God who loved me and had the power to help me lead an overcoming life. That is the underlying message of the book and the hope that I am committed to try to impart. My truth is that with God's help you do not have to carry the "load" until you die. It is exhausting to have to continue define and redefine some sort of rule of engagement that helps you maintain equilibrium and sanity in a world of CHAOS.

We are not supposed to handle this life and its sorrows, disappointments, hurts and challenges on our own.

Chaos Eaters

We have resources available through faith and the spirit of reconciliation which is the message of grace inherent the Gospel message of Jesus.

That is my truth, my fulcrum, my bedrock, my true North and the compass of my journey. It has served me well and allowed me to overcome CHAOS in my own life. While those things from my past and the influences found there continue to try to exert themselves in what I think of as a sort of "Phantom limb" experience.

That departed appendage twitches sometimes but it is no longer attached to me. Do I occasionally feel rejected or shamed and depressed? Yes! But those experiences and lenses have become less and less powerful over time and I no longer define myself in those terms and I no longer am tempted to carry the load when they present themselves. I have learned to "cast my cares upon the Lord and He has sustained me."

What a journey it continues to be! I no longer feel like Sisyphus pushing that stone up the mountain in futility, knowing it will always roll back on me. I am convinced that the gods are not against me, in fact, I know that" If my God is for me, who can be against me" and I approach each day and the CHAOS that still wants to rule my heart with a confidence not in my own efforts or strength but a reliance on the active hand of God in my own life.

And *that* is a wonderful thing!

RESOURCES

In my personal journey I have found wisdom, counsel, and part of the answers to the puzzle in many places. I want to cite a few of these here because I want you to have additional resources for your continued growth. I also want to give credit where credit is due; we all stand on the shoulders of giants. The authors and topics listed below have all made an impact on my life's journey; enjoy the adventure!

- The Bible
- Florence Littauer: Personality Plus
- Dr. Gershon Kaufman: Coming Out of Shame
- Janet Geringer Woititz: Adult Children of Alcoholics
- John Bevere: The Bait of Satan
- James G. Friesen, E. James Wilder, Anne M. Bierling, Rick Koepcke, Maribeth Poole: THE LIFE MODEL:
- Living from the Heart Jesus Gave You
- Fred Davis; Beyond Recovery
- Neil T. Anderson: The Bondage Breaker
- John and Paula Sandford: The Transformation of the Inner Man
- John Bradshaw: HOMECOMING: Reclaiming and Championing Your Inner Child
- Dr. Tim Clinton and Dr. Gary Sibcy: ATTACHMENTS: Why You Love, Feel and Act the Way You Do
- Watchman Nee: The Spiritual Man